P9-CAO-084

Books by Ernest Hemingway

THE ENDURING HEMINGWAY

THE NICK ADAMS STORIES

ISLANDS IN THE STREAM

THE FIFTH COLUMN AND FOUR STORIES
    OF THE SPANISH CIVIL WAR

BY-LINE: ERNEST HEMINGWAY

A MOVEABLE FEAST

THREE NOVELS

THE SNOWS OF KILIMANJARO AND OTHER STORIES

THE HEMINGWAY READER

THE OLD MAN AND THE SEA

ACROSS THE RIVER AND INTO THE TREES

FOR WHOM THE BELL TOLLS

THE SHORT STORIES OF ERNEST HEMINGWAY

TO HAVE AND HAVE NOT

GREEN HILLS OF AFRICA

WINNER TAKE NOTHING

DEATH IN THE AFTERNOON

IN OUR TIME

A FAREWELL TO ARMS

MEN WITHOUT WOMEN

THE SUN ALSO RISES

THE TORRENTS OF SPRING

A Moveable Feast

ERNEST HEMINGWAY

A Moveable Feast

If you are lucky enough to have lived
in Paris as a young man, then wherever you
go for the rest of your life, it stays with
you, for Paris is a moveable feast.

ERNEST HEMINGWAY
to a friend, 1950

CHARLES SCRIBNER'S SONS, *New York*

Copyright © 1964 Ernest Hemingway Ltd.

This book published simultaneously in the
United States of America and in Canada—
Copyright under the Berne Convention

*All rights reserved. No part of this book
may be reproduced in any form without
the permission of Charles Scribner's Sons.*

1 3 5 7 9 11 13 15 17 19 K/P 20 18 16 14 12 10 8 6 4 2

PICTURE ACKNOWLEDGMENTS

1, 2 and 9. Family Collection
3. Collection of Man Ray
4. Copyright Estate of Sylvia Beach. From the Collection of Sylvia Beach,
   Paris
5. Photograph by Gisèle Freund, Paris
6. From the Sylvia Beach Collection, State University of New York at
   Buffalo
7. Collection of Man Ray
8. Courtesy of Mrs. Samuel J. Lanahan

PRINTED IN THE UNITED STATES OF AMERICA

ISBN 0-684-17996-2

Library of Congress Catalog Card Number 64-15441

Contents

Preface

For reasons sufficient to the writer, many places, people, observations and impressions have been left out of this book. Some were secrets and some were known by everyone and everyone has written about them and will doubtless write more.

There is no mention of the Stade Anastasie where the boxers served as waiters at the tables set out under the trees and the ring was in the garden. Nor of training with Larry Gains, nor the great twenty-round fights at the Cirque d'Hiver. Nor of such good friends as Charlie Sweeny, Bill Bird and Mike Strater, nor of André Masson and Miro. There is no mention of our voyages to the Black Forest or of our one-day explorations of the forests that we loved around Paris. It would be fine if all these were in this book but we will have to do without them for now.

If the reader prefers, this book may be regarded as fiction. But there is always the chance that such a book of fiction may throw some light on what has been written as fact.

Ernest Hemingway

San Francisco de Paula, Cuba
1960

Note

Ernest started writing this book in Cuba in the autumn of 1957, worked on it in Ketchum, Idaho, in the winter of 1958–59, took it with him to Spain when we went there in April, 1959, and brought it back with him to Cuba and then to Ketchum late that fall. He finished the book in the spring of 1960 in Cuba, after having put it aside to write another book, *The Dangerous Summer*, about the violent rivalry between Antonio Ordonez and Luis Miguel Dominguin in the bull rings of Spain in 1959. He made some revisions of this book in the fall in 1960 in Ketchum. It concerns the years 1921 to 1926 in Paris.

M. H.

A Good Café
on the Place St.-Michel

THEN there was the bad weather. It would come in one day when the fall was over. We would have to shut the windows in the night against the rain and the cold wind would strip the leaves from the trees in the Place Contrescarpe. The leaves lay sodden in the rain and the wind drove the rain against the big green autobus at the terminal and the Café des Amateurs was crowded and the windows misted over from the heat and the smoke inside. It was a sad, evilly run café where the drunkards of the quarter crowded together and I kept away from it because of the smell of dirty bodies and the sour smell of drunkenness. The men and women who frequented the Amateurs stayed drunk all of the time, or all of the time they could afford it, mostly on wine which they bought by the half-liter or liter. Many strangely named apéritifs were advertised, but few people could afford them except as a foundation to build their wine drunks on. The women drunkards were called *poivrottes* which meant female rummies.

The Café des Amateurs was the cesspool of the rue Mouffetard, that wonderful narrow crowded market street which led into the Place Contrescarpe. The squat toilets of the old apartment houses, one by the side of the stairs on each floor with the two cleated cement shoe-shaped elevations on each side of the aperture so a *locataire* would not slip, emptied into cesspools which were emptied by pumping into horse-drawn tank wagons at night. In the summer time, with all windows open, we would hear the pumping and the odor was very strong. The tank wagons were painted brown and saffron color and in the moonlight when they worked the rue Cardinal Lemoine their wheeled, horse-drawn cylinders looked like Braque paintings. No one emptied the Café des Amateurs though, and its yellowed poster stating the terms and penalties of the law against public drunkenness was as flyblown and disregarded as its clients were constant and ill-smelling.

All of the sadness of the city came suddenly with the first cold rains of winter, and there were no more tops to the high white houses as you walked but only the wet blackness of the street and the closed doors of the small shops, the herb sellers, the stationery and the newspaper shops, the midwife—second class—and the hotel where Verlaine had died where I had a room on the top floor where I worked.

It was either six or eight flights up to the top floor and it was very cold and I knew how much it would cost for a bundle of small twigs, three wire-wrapped packets of short, half-pencil length pieces of split pine to catch fire from the twigs, and then the bundle of half-dried lengths of hard wood that I must buy to make a fire that would warm the room. So I went to the far side of the street to look up at the roof in the rain and see if any chimneys were going, and how the smoke blew. There was no smoke and I thought about how the chimney would be cold and might not draw and of the room possibly filling with smoke, and the fuel wasted, and the money gone with it, and I walked on in the rain. I walked down past the Lycée Henri Quatre and the ancient church of St.-Étienne-du-Mont and the windswept Place du Panthéon and cut in for shelter to the right and finally came out on the lee side of the

Boulevard St.-Michel and worked on down it past the Cluny and the Boulevard St.-Germain until I came to a good café that I knew on the Place St.-Michel.

It was a pleasant café, warm and clean and friendly, and I hung up my old waterproof on the coat rack to dry and put my worn and weathered felt hat on the rack above the bench and ordered a *café au lait*. The waiter brought it and I took out a notebook from the pocket of the coat and a pencil and started to write. I was writing about up in Michigan and since it was a wild, cold, blowing day it was that sort of day in the story. I had already seen the end of fall come through boyhood, youth and young manhood, and in one place you could write about it better than in another. That was called transplanting yourself, I thought, and it could be as necessary with people as with other sorts of growing things. But in the story the boys were drinking and this made me thirsty and I ordered a rum St. James. This tasted wonderful on the cold day and I kept on writing, feeling very well and feeling the good Martinique rum warm me all through my body and my spirit.

A girl came in the café and sat by herself at a table near the window. She was very pretty with a face fresh as a newly minted coin if they minted coins in smooth flesh with rain-freshened skin, and her hair was black as a crow's wing and cut sharply and diagonally across her cheek.

I looked at her and she disturbed me and made me very excited. I wished I could put her in the story, or anywhere, but she had placed herself so she could watch the street and the entry and I knew she was waiting for someone. So I went on writing.

The story was writing itself and I was having a hard time keeping up with it. I ordered another rum St. James and I watched the girl whenever I looked up, or when I sharpened the pencil with a pencil sharpener with the shavings curling into the saucer under my drink.

I've seen you, beauty, and you belong to me now, whoever you are waiting for and if I never see you again, I thought. You belong to me and all Paris belongs to me and I belong to this notebook and this pencil.

Then I went back to writing and I entered far into the story and was lost in it. I was writing it now and it was not writing itself and I did not look up nor know anything about the time nor think where I was nor order any more rum St. James. I was tired of rum St. James without thinking about it. Then the story was finished and I was very tired. I read the last paragraph and then I looked up and looked for the girl and she had gone. I hope she's gone with a good man, I thought. But I felt sad.

I closed up the story in the notebook and put it in my inside pocket and I asked the waiter for a dozen *portugaises* and a half-carafe of the dry white wine they had there. After writing a story I was always empty and both sad and happy, as though I had made love, and I was sure this was a very good story although I would not know truly how good until I read it over the next day.

As I ate the oysters with their strong taste of the sea and their faint metallic taste that the cold white wine washed away, leaving only the sea taste and the succulent texture, and as I drank their cold liquid from each shell and washed it down with the crisp taste of the wine, I lost the empty feeling and began to be happy and to make plans.

Now that the bad weather had come, we could leave Paris for a while for a place where this rain would be snow coming down through the pines and covering the road and the high hillsides and at an altitude where we would hear it creak as we walked home at night. Below Les Avants there was a chalet where the pension was wonderful and where we would be together and have our books and at night be warm in bed together with the windows open and the stars bright. That was where we could go. Traveling third class on the train was not expensive. The pension cost very little more than we spent in Paris.

I would give up the room in the hotel where I wrote and there was only the rent of 74 rue Cardinal Lemoine which was nominal. I had written journalism for Toronto and the checks for that were due. I could write that anywhere under any circumstances and we had money to make the trip.

Maybe away from Paris I could write about Paris as in Paris I could write about Michigan. I did not know it was too early for that because I did not know Paris well enough. But that was how it worked out eventually. Anyway we would go if my wife wanted to, and I finished the oysters and the wine and paid my score in the café and made it the shortest way back up the Montagne Ste. Geneviève through the rain, that was now only local weather and not something that changed your life, to the flat at the top of the hill.

"I think it would be wonderful, Tatie," my wife said. She had a gently modeled face and her eyes and her smile lighted up at decisions as though they were rich presents. "When should we leave?"

"Whenever you want."

"Oh, I want to right away. Didn't you know?"

"Maybe it will be fine and clear when we come back. It can be very fine when it is clear and cold."

"I'm sure it will be," she said. "Weren't you good to think of going, too."

Miss Stein Instructs

WHEN we came back to Paris it was clear and cold and lovely. The city had accommodated itself to winter, there was good wood for sale at the wood and coal place across our street, and there were braziers outside of many of the good cafés so that you could keep warm on the terraces. Our own apartment was warm and cheerful. We burned *boulets* which were molded, egg-shaped lumps of coal dust, on the wood fire, and on the streets the winter light was beautiful. Now you were accustomed to see the bare trees against the sky and you walked on the fresh-washed gravel paths through the Luxembourg gardens in the clear sharp wind. The trees were sculpture without their leaves when you were reconciled to them, and the winter winds blew across the surfaces of the ponds and the fountains blew in the bright light. All the distances were short now since we had been in the mountains.

Because of the change in altitude I did not notice the grade of the hills except with pleasure, and the climb up to the top floor of the hotel where I worked, in a room that looked across all the roofs and the chimneys of the high hill of the quarter, was a pleasure. The fireplace drew well in the room and it was warm and pleasant to work. I brought mandarines and roasted chestnuts to the room in paper packets and peeled and ate the small tangerine-like oranges and threw their skins and spat their seeds in the fire when I ate them and roasted chestnuts when I was hungry. I was always hungry with the walking and the cold and the working. Up in the room I had a bottle of kirsch that we had brought back from the mountains and I took a drink of kirsch when I would get toward the end of a story or toward the end of the day's work. When I was through working for the day I put away the notebook, or the paper, in the drawer of the table and put any mandarines that were left in my pocket. They would freeze if they were left in the room at night.

It was wonderful to walk down the long flights of stairs knowing that I'd had good luck working. I always worked until I had something done and I always stopped when I knew what was going to happen next. That way I could be sure of going on the next day. But sometimes when I was starting a new story and I could not get it going, I would sit in front of the fire and squeeze the peel of the little oranges into the edge of the flame and watch the sputter of blue that they made. I would stand and look out over the roofs of Paris and think, "Do not worry. You have always written before and you will write now. All you have to do is write one true sentence. Write the truest sentence that you know." So finally I would write one true sentence, and then go on from there. It was easy then because there was always one true sentence that I knew or had seen or had heard someone say. If I started to write elaborately, or like someone introducing or presenting something, I found that I could cut that scrollwork or ornament out and throw it away and start with the first true simple declarative sentence I had written. Up in that room I decided that I would write one story about each thing that I knew about. I was trying to do this all the time I was writing, and it was good and severe discipline.

It was in that room too that I learned not to think about anything that I was writing from the time I stopped writing until I started again the next day. That way my subconscious would be working on it and at the same time I would be listening to other people and noticing everything, I hoped; learning, I hoped; and I would read so that I would not think about my work and make myself impotent to do it. Going down the stairs when I had worked well, and that needed luck as well as discipline, was a wonderful feeling and I was free then to walk anywhere in Paris.

If I walked down by different streets to the Jardin du Luxembourg in the afternoon I could walk through the gardens and then go to the Musée du Luxembourg where the great paintings were that have now mostly been transferred to the Louvre and the Jeu de Paume. I went there nearly every day for the Cézannes and to see the Manets and the Monets and the other Impressionists that I had first come to know about in the Art Institute at Chicago. I was learning something from the painting of Cézanne that made writing simple true sentences far from enough to make the stories have the dimensions that I was trying to put in them. I was learning very much from him but I was not articulate enough to explain it to anyone. Besides it was a secret. But if the light was gone in the Luxembourg I would walk up through the gardens and stop in at the studio apartment where Gertrude Stein lived at 27 rue de Fleurus.

My wife and I had called on Miss Stein, and she and the friend who lived with her had been very cordial and friendly and we had loved the big studio with the great paintings. It was like one of the best rooms in the finest museum except there was a big fireplace and it was warm and comfortable and they gave you good things to eat and tea and natural distilled liqueurs made from purple plums, yellow plums or wild raspberries. These were fragrant, colorless alcohols served from cut-glass carafes in small glasses and whether they were *quetsche, mirabelle* or *framboise* they all tasted like the fruits they came from, converted into a controlled fire on your tongue that warmed you and loosened it.

Miss Stein was very big but not tall and was heavily built like a peasant woman. She had beautiful eyes and a strong German-Jewish face that also could have been Friulano and she reminded me of a northern Italian peasant woman with her clothes, her mobile face and her lovely, thick, alive immigrant hair which she wore put up in the same way she had probably worn it in college. She talked all the time and at first it was about people and places.

Her companion had a very pleasant voice, was small, very dark, with her hair cut like Joan of Arc in the Boutet de Monvel illustrations and had a very hooked nose. She was working on a piece of needlepoint when we first met them and she worked on this and saw to the food and drink and talked to my wife. She made one conversation and listened to two and often interrupted the one she was not making. Afterwards she explained to me that she always talked to the wives. The wives, my wife and I felt, were tolerated. But we liked Miss Stein and her friend, although the friend was frightening. The paintings and the cakes and the *eau-de-vie* were truly wonderful. They seemed to like us too and treated us as though we were very good, well mannered and promising children and I felt that they forgave us for being in love and being married

—time would fix that—and when my wife invited them to tea, they accepted.

When they came to our flat they seemed to like us even more; but perhaps that was because the place was so small and we were much closer together. Miss Stein sat on the bed that was on the floor and asked to see the stories I had written and she said that she liked them except one called "Up in Michigan."

"It's good," she said. "That's not the question at all. But it is *inaccrochable*. That means it is like a picture that a painter paints and then he cannot hang it when he has a show and nobody will buy it because they cannot hang it either."

"But what if it is not dirty but it is only that you are trying to use words that people would actually use? That are the only words that can make the story come true and that you must use them? You have to use them."

"But you don't get the point at all," she said. "You mustn't write anything that is *inaccrochable*. There is no point in it. It's wrong and it's silly."

She herself wanted to be published in the *Atlantic Monthly*, she told me, and she would be. She told me that I was not a good enough writer to be published there or in *The Saturday Evening Post* but that I might be some new sort of writer in my own way but the first thing to remember was not to write stories that were *inaccrochable*. I did not argue about this nor try to explain again what I was trying to do about conversation. That was my own business and it was much more interesting to listen. That afternoon she told us, too, how to buy pictures.

"You can either buy clothes or buy pictures," she said. "It's that simple. No one who is not very rich can do both. Pay no attention to your clothes and no attention at all to the mode, and buy your clothes for comfort and durability, and you will have the clothes money to buy pictures."

"But even if I never bought any more clothing ever," I said, "I wouldn't have enough money to buy the Picassos that I want."

"No. He's out of your range. You have to buy the people of your own age—of your own military service group. You'll know them. You'll meet them around the quarter. There are always good new serious painters. But it's not you buying clothes so much. It's your wife always. It's women's clothes that are expensive."

I saw my wife trying not to look at the strange, steerage clothes that Miss Stein wore and she was successful. When they left we were still popular, I thought, and we were asked to come again to 27 rue de Fleurus.

It was later on that I was asked to come to the studio any time after five in the winter time. I had met Miss Stein in the Luxembourg. I cannot remember whether she was walking her dog or not, nor whether she had a dog then. I know that I was walking myself, since we could not afford a dog nor even a cat then, and the only cats I knew were in the cafés or small restaurants or the great cats that I admired in concierges' windows. Later I often met Miss Stein with her dog in the Luxembourg gardens; but I think this time was before she had one.

But I accepted her invitation, dog or no dog, and had taken to stopping in at the studio, and she always gave me the natural *eau-de-vie*, insisting on my refilling my glass, and I looked at the pictures and we talked. The pictures were exciting and the talk was very good. She talked, mostly, and she told me about modern pictures and about painters—more about them as people than as painters—and she talked about her work. She showed me the many volumes of manuscript that she had written and that her companion typed each day. Writing every day made her happy, but as I got to know her better I found that for her to keep happy it was necessary that this steady daily output, which varied with her energy, be published and that she receive recognition.

This had not become an acute situation when I first knew her, since she had published three stories that were intelligible to anyone. One of these stories, "Melanctha," was very good and good samples of her experimental writing had been published in book form and had been well praised by critics who had met her or known her. She had such a personality that when she wished to win anyone over to her side she would not be resisted, and critics who met her and saw her pictures took on trust writing of hers that they could not understand because of their enthusiasm for her as a person, and because of their confidence in her judgment. She had also discovered many truths about rhythms and the uses of words in repetition that were valid and valuable and she talked well about them.

But she disliked the drudgery of revision and the obligation to make her writing intelligible, although she needed to have publication and official acceptance, especially for the unbelievably long book called *The Making of Americans.*

This book began magnificently, went on very well for a long way with great stretches of great brilliance and then went on endlessly in repetitions that a more conscientious and less lazy writer would have put in the waste basket. I came to know it very well as I got—forced, perhaps would be the word—Ford Madox Ford to publish it in *The Transatlantic Review* serially, knowing that it would outrun the life of the review. For publication in the review I had to read all of Miss Stein's proof for her as this was a work which gave her no happiness.

On this cold afternoon when I had come past the concierge's lodge and the cold courtyard to the warmth of the studio, all that was years ahead. On this day Miss Stein was instructing me about sex. By that time we liked each other very much and I had already learned that everything I did not understand probably had something to it. Miss Stein thought that I was too uneducated about sex and I must admit that I had certain prejudices against homosexuality since I knew its more primitive aspects. I knew it was why you carried a knife and would use it when you were in the company of tramps when you were a boy in the days when wolves was not a slang term for men obsessed by the pursuit of women. I knew many *inaccrochable* terms and phrases from Kansas City days and the mores of different parts of that city, Chicago and the lake boats. Under questioning I tried to tell Miss Stein that when you were a boy and moved in the company of men, you had to be prepared to kill a man, know how to do it and really know that you would do it in order not to be interfered with. That term was *accrochable*. If you knew you would kill, other people sensed it very quickly and you were let alone; but there were certain situations you could not allow yourself to be forced into or trapped into. I could have expressed myself more vividly by using an *inaccrochable* phrase that wolves used on the lake boats, "Oh gash may be fine but one eye for mine." But I was always careful of my language with Miss Stein even when true phrases might have clarified or better expressed a prejudice.

"Yes, yes, Hemingway," she said. "But you were living in a milieu of criminals and perverts."

I did not want to argue that, although I thought that I had lived in a world as it was and there were all kinds of people in it and I tried to understand them, although some of them I could not like and some I still hated.

"But what about the old man with beautiful manners and a great name who came to the hospital in Italy and brought me a bottle of Marsala or Campari and behaved perfectly, and then one day I would have to tell the nurse never to let that man into the room again?" I asked.

"Those people are sick and cannot help themselves and you should pity them."

"Should I pity so and so?" I asked. I gave his name but he delights so in giving it himself that I feel there is no need to give it for him.

"No. He's vicious. He's a corrupter and he's truly vicious."

"But he's supposed to be a good writer."

"He's not," she said. "He's just a showman and he corrupts for the pleasure of corruption and he leads people into other vicious practices as well. Drugs, for example."

"And in Milan the man I'm to pity was not trying to corrupt me?"

"Don't be silly. How could he hope to corrupt you? Do you corrupt a boy like you, who drinks alcohol, with a bottle of

Marsala? No, he was a pitiful old man who could not help what he was doing. He was sick and he could not help it and you should pity him."

"I did at the time," I said. "But I was disappointed because he had such beautiful manners."

I took another sip of the *eau-de-vie* and pitied the old man and looked at Picasso's nude of the girl with the basket of flowers. I had not started the conversation and thought it had become a little dangerous. There were almost never any pauses in a conversation with Miss Stein, but we had paused and there was something she wanted to tell me and I filled my glass.

"You know nothing about any of this really, Hemingway," she said. "You've met known criminals and sick people and vicious people. The main thing is that the act male homosexuals commit is ugly and repugnant and afterwards they are disgusted with themselves. They drink and take drugs, to palliate this, but they are disgusted with the act and they are always changing partners and cannot be really happy."

"I see."

"In women it is the opposite. They do nothing that they are disgusted by and nothing that is repulsive and afterwards they are happy and they can lead happy lives together."

"I see," I said. "But what about so and so?"

"She's vicious," Miss Stein said. "She's truly vicious, so she can never be happy except with new people. She corrupts people."

"I understand."

"You're sure you understand?"

There were so many things to understand in those days and

I was glad when we talked about something else. The park was closed so I had to walk down along it to the rue de Vaugirard and around the lower end of the park. It was sad when the park was closed and locked and I was sad walking around it instead of through it and in a hurry to get home to the rue Cardinal Lemoine. The day had started out so brightly too. I would have to work hard tomorrow. Work could cure almost anything, I believed then, and I believe now. Then all I had to be cured of, I decided Miss Stein felt, was youth and loving my wife. I was not at all sad when I got home to the rue Cardinal Lemoine and told my newly acquired knowledge to my wife. In the night we were happy with our own knowledge we already had and other new knowledge we had acquired in the mountains.

"Une Génération Perdue"

It was easy to get into the habit of stopping in at 27 rue de Fleurus late in the afternoon for the warmth and the great pictures and the conversation. Often Miss Stein would have no guests and she was always very friendly and for a long time she was affectionate. When I had come back from trips that I had made to the different political conferences or to the Near East or Germany for the Canadian paper and the news services that I worked for she wanted me to tell her about all the amusing details. There were funny parts always and she liked them and also what the Germans call gallows-humor stories. She wanted to know the gay part of how the world was going; never the real, never the bad.

I was young and not gloomy and there were always strange and comic things that happened in the worst time and Miss Stein liked to hear these. The other things I did not talk of and wrote by myself.

When I had not come back from any trips and would stop in at the rue de Fleurus after working I would try sometimes to get Miss Stein to talk about books. When I was writing, it was necessary for me to read after I had written. If you kept thinking about it, you would lose the thing that you were writing before you could go on with it the next day. It was necessary to get exercise, to be tired in the body, and it was very good to make love with whom you loved. That was better than anything. But afterwards, when you were empty, it was necessary to read in order not to think or worry about your work until you could do it again. I had learned already never to empty the well of my writing, but always to stop when there was still something there in the deep part of the well, and let it refill at night from the springs that fed it.

To keep my mind off writing sometimes after I had worked I would read writers who were writing then, such as Aldous Huxley, D. H. Lawrence or any who had books published that I could get from Sylvia Beach's library or find along the quais.

"Huxley is a dead man," Miss Stein said. "Why do you want to read a dead man? Can't you see he is dead?"

I could not see, then, that he was a dead man and I said that his books amused me and kept me from thinking.

"You should only read what is truly good or what is frankly bad."

"I've been reading truly good books all winter and all last winter and I'll read them next winter, and I don't like frankly bad books."

"Why do you read this trash? It is inflated trash, Hemingway. By a dead man."

"I like to see what they are writing," I said. "And it keeps my mind off me doing it."

"Who else do you read now?"

"D. H. Lawrence," I said. "He wrote some very good short stories, one called 'The Prussian Officer.'"

"I tried to read his novels. He's impossible. He's pathetic and preposterous. He writes like a sick man."

"I liked *Sons and Lovers* and *The White Peacock*," I said. "Maybe that not so well. I couldn't read *Women in Love*."

"If you don't want to read what is bad, and want to read something that will hold your interest and is marvelous in its own way, you should read Marie Belloc Lowndes."

I had never heard of her, and Miss Stein loaned me *The Lodger*, that marvelous story of Jack the Ripper and another book about murder at a place outside Paris that could only be Enghien les Bains. They were both splendid after-work books, the people credible and the action and the terror never false. They were perfect for reading after you had worked and I read all the Mrs. Belloc Lowndes that there was. But there was only so much and none as good as the first two and I never found anything as good for that empty time of day or night until the first fine Simenon books came out.

I think Miss Stein would have liked the good Simenons—the first one I read was either *L'Ecluse Numéro 1*, or *La Maison du Canal*—but I am not sure because when I knew Miss Stein she did not like to read French although she loved to speak it. Janet Flanner gave me the first two Simenons I ever read. She loved to read French and she had read Simenon when he was a crime reporter.

In the three or four years that we were good friends I cannot remember Gertrude Stein ever speaking well of any writer who had not written favorably about her work or done something to advance her career except for Ronald Firbank and, later, Scott Fitzgerald. When I first met her she did not speak of Sherwood Anderson as a writer but spoke glowingly of him as a man and of his great, beautiful, warm Italian eyes and of his kindness and his charm. I did not care about his great beautiful warm Italian eyes but I liked some of his short stories very much. They were simply written and sometimes beautifully written and he knew the people he was writing about and cared deeply for them. Miss Stein did not want to talk about his stories but always about him as a person.

"What about his novels?" I asked her. She did not want to talk about Anderson's works any more than she would talk about Joyce. If you brought up Joyce twice, you would not be invited back. It was like mentioning one general favorably to another general. You learned not to do it the first time you made the mistake. You could always mention a general, though, that the general you were talking to had beaten. The general you were talking to would praise the beaten general greatly and go happily into detail on how he had beaten him.

Anderson's stories were too good to make happy conversation. I was prepared to tell Miss Stein how strangely poor his novels were, but this would have been bad too because it was criticizing one of her most loyal supporters. When he wrote a novel finally called *Dark Laughter*, so terribly bad, silly and affected that I could not keep from criticizing it in a parody,* Miss Stein was very angry. I had attacked someone that was a part of her apparatus. But for a long time before that she was not angry. She, herself, began to praise Sherwood lavishly after he had cracked up as a writer.

She was angry at Ezra Pound because he had sat down too quickly on a small, fragile and, doubtless, uncomfortable chair, that it is quite possible he had been given on purpose, and had either cracked or broken it. That he was a great poet and a gentle and generous man and could have accommodated himself in a normal-size chair was not considered. The reasons for her dislike of Ezra, skillfully and maliciously put, were invented years later.

The Torrents of Spring.

It was when we had come back from Canada and were living in the rue Notre-Dame-des-Champs and Miss Stein and I were still good friends that Miss Stein made the remark about the lost generation. She had some ignition trouble with the old Model T Ford she then drove and the young man who worked in the garage and had served in the last year of the war had not been adept, or perhaps had not broken the priority of other vehicles, in repairing Miss Stein's Ford. Anyway he had not been *sérieux* and had been corrected severely by the *patron* of the garage after Miss Stein's protest. The *patron* had said to him, "You are all a *génération perdue*."

"That's what you are. That's what you all are," Miss Stein said. "All of you young people who served in the war. You are a lost generation."

"Really?" I said.

"You are," she insisted. "You have no respect for anything. You drink yourselves to death. . . ."

"Was the young mechanic drunk?" I asked.

"Of course not."

"Have you ever seen me drunk?"

"No. But your friends are drunk."

"I've been drunk," I said. "But I don't come here drunk."

"Of course not. I didn't say that."

"The boy's *patron* was probably drunk by eleven o'clock in the morning," I said. "That's why he makes such lovely phrases."

"Don't argue with me, Hemingway," Miss Stein said. "It does no good at all. You're all a lost generation, exactly as the garage keeper said."

Later when I wrote my first novel I tried to balance Miss Stein's quotation from the garage keeper with one from Ecclesiastes. But that night walking home I thought about the boy in the garage and if he had ever been hauled in one of those vehicles when they were converted to ambulances. I remembered how they used to burn out their brakes going down the mountain roads with a full load of wounded and braking in low and finally using the reverse, and how the last ones were driven over the mountainside empty, so they could be replaced by big Fiats with a good H-shift and metal-to-metal brakes. I thought of Miss Stein and Sherwood Anderson and egotism and mental laziness versus discipline and I thought who is calling who a lost generation? Then as I was getting up to the Closerie des Lilas with the light on my old friend, the statue of Marshal Ney with his sword out and the shadows of the trees on the bronze, and he alone there and nobody behind him and what a fiasco he'd made of Waterloo, I thought that all generations were lost by something and always had been and always would be and I stopped at the Lilas to keep the statue company and drank a cold beer before going home to the flat over the sawmill. But sitting there with the beer, watching the statue and remembering how many days Ney had fought, personally, with the rear-guard on the retreat from Moscow that Napoleon had ridden away from in the coach with Caulaincourt, I thought of what a warm and affectionate friend Miss Stein had been and how beautifully she had spoken of Apollinaire and of his death on the day of the Armistice in 1918 with the crowd shouting "*à bas Guillaume*" and Apollinaire, in his delirium, thinking they were crying against him, and I thought, I will do my best to serve her and see she gets justice for the good work she had done as long as I can, so help me God and Mike Ney. But the hell with her lost-generation talk and all the dirty, easy labels. When I got home and into the courtyard and upstairs and saw my wife and my son and his cat, F. Puss, all of them happy and a fire in the fireplace, I said to my wife, "You know, Gertrude *is* nice, anyway."

"Of course, Tatie."

"But she does talk a lot of rot sometimes."

"I never hear her," my wife said. "I'm a wife. It's her friend that talks to me."

Shakespeare and Company

In those days there was no money to buy books. I borrowed books from the rental library of Shakespeare and Company, which was the library and bookstore of Sylvia Beach at 12 rue de l'Odéon. On a cold windswept street, this was a warm, cheerful place with a big stove in winter, tables and shelves of books, new books in the window, and photographs on the wall of famous writers both dead and living. The photographs all looked like snapshots and even the dead writers looked as though they had really been alive. Sylvia had a lively, sharply sculptured face, brown eyes that were as alive as a small animal's and as gay as a young girl's, and wavy brown hair that was brushed back from her fine forehead and cut thick below her ears and at the line of the collar of the brown velvet jacket she wore. She had pretty legs and she was kind, cheerful and interested, and loved to make jokes and gossip. No one that I ever knew was nicer to me.

I was very shy when I first went into the bookshop and I did not have enough money on me to join the rental library. She told me I could pay the deposit any time I had the money and made me out a card and said I could take as many books as I wished.

There was no reason for her to trust me. She did not know me and the address I had given her, 74 rue Cardinal Lemoine, could not have been a poorer one. But she was delightful and charming and welcoming and behind her, as high as the wall and stretching out into the back room which gave onto the inner court of the building, were shelves and shelves of the wealth of the library.

I started with Turgenev and took the two volumes of *A Sportsman's Sketches* and an early book of D. H. Lawrence, I think it was *Sons and Lovers,* and Sylvia told me to take more books if I wanted. I chose the Constance Garnett edition of *War and Peace,* and *The Gambler and Other Stories* by Dostoyevsky.

"You won't be back very soon if you read all that," Sylvia said.

"I'll be back to pay," I said. "I have some money in the flat."

"I didn't mean that," she said. "You pay whenever it's convenient."

"When does Joyce come in?" I asked.

"If he comes in, it's usually very late in the afternoon," she said. "Haven't you ever seen him?"

"We've seen him at Michaud's eating with his family," I said. "But it's not polite to look at people when they are eating, and Michaud's is expensive."

"Do you eat at home?"

"Mostly now," I said. "We have a good cook."

"There aren't any restaurants in your immediate quarter, are there?"

"No. How did you know?"

"Larbaud lived there," she said. "He liked it very much except for that."

"The nearest good cheap place to eat is over by the Panthéon."

"I don't know that quarter. We eat at home. You and your wife must come sometime."

"Wait until you see if I pay you," I said. "But thank you very much."

"Don't read too fast," she said.

Home in the rue Cardinal Lemoine was a two-room flat that had no hot water and no inside toilet facilities except an antiseptic container, not uncomfortable to anyone who was used to a Michigan outhouse. With a fine view and a good mattress and springs for a comfortable bed on the floor, and pictures we liked on the walls, it was a cheerful, gay flat. When I got there with the books I told my wife about the wonderful place I had found.

"But Tatie, you must go by this afternoon and pay," she said.

"Sure I will," I said. "We'll both go. And then we'll walk down by the river and along the quais."

"Let's walk down the rue de Seine and look in all the galleries and in the windows of the shops."

"Sure. We can walk anywhere and we can stop at some new café where we don't know anyone and nobody knows us and have a drink."

"We can have two drinks."

"Then we can eat somewhere."

"No. Don't forget we have to pay the library."

"We'll come home and eat here and we'll have a lovely meal and drink Beaune from the co-operative you can see right out of the window there with the price of the Beaune on the window. And afterwards we'll read and then go to bed and make love."

"And we'll never love anyone else but each other."

"No. Never."

"What a lovely afternoon and evening. Now we'd better have lunch."

"I'm very hungry," I said. "I worked at the café on a *café crème*."

"How did it go, Tatie?"

"I think all right. I hope so. What do we have for lunch?"

"Little radishes, and good *foie de veau* with mashed potatoes and an endive salad. Apple tart."

"And we're going to have all the books in the world to read and when we go on trips we can take them."

"Would that be honest?"

"Sure."

"Does she have Henry James too?"

"Sure."

"My," she said. "We're lucky that you found the place."

"We're always lucky," I said and like a fool I did not knock on wood. There was wood everywhere in that apartment to knock on too.

People of the Seine

THERE were many ways of walking down to the river from the top of the rue Cardinal Lemoine. The shortest one was straight down the street but it was steep and it brought you out, after you hit the flat part and crossed the busy traffic of the beginning of the Boulevard St.-Germain, onto a dull part where there was a bleak, windy stretch of river bank with the Halle aux Vins on your right. This was not like any other Paris market but was a sort of bonded warehouse where wine was stored against the payment of taxes and was as cheerless from the outside as a military depot or a prison camp.

Across the branch of the Seine was the Île St.-Louis with the narrow streets and the old, tall, beautiful houses, and you could go over there or you could turn left and walk along the quais with the length of the Ile St.-Louis and then Notre-Dame and Île de la Cité opposite as you walked.

In the bookstalls along the quais you could sometimes find American books that had just been published for sale very cheap. The Tour D'Argent restaurant had a few rooms above the restaurant that they rented in those days, giving the people who lived there a discount in the restaurant, and if the people who lived there left any books behind there was a bookstall not far along the quai where the *valet de chambre* sold them and you could buy them from the proprietress for a very few francs. She had no confidence in books written in English, paid almost nothing for them, and sold them for a small and quick profit.

"Are they any good?" she asked me after we had become friends.

"Sometimes one is."

"How can anyone tell?"

"I can tell when I read them."

"But still it is a form of gambling. And how many people can read English?"

"Save them for me and let me look them over."

"No. I can't save them. You don't pass regularly. You stay away too long at a time. I have to sell them as soon as I can. No one can tell if they are worthless. If they turn out to be worthless, I would never sell them."

"How do you tell a valuable French book?"

"First there are the pictures. Then it is a question of the quality of the pictures. Then it is the binding. If a book is good, the owner will have it bound properly. All books in English are bound, but bound badly. There is no way of judging them."

After that bookstall near the Tour D'Argent there were no others that sold American and English books until the quai des Grands Augustins. There were several from there on to beyond the quai Voltaire that sold books they bought from employees of the left bank hotels and especially the Hotel Voltaire which had a wealthier clientele than most. One day I asked another woman stall-keeper who was a friend of mine if the owners ever sold the books.

"No," she said. "They are all thrown away. That is why one knows they have no value."

"Friends give them to them to read on the boats."

"Doubtless," she said. "They must leave many on the boats."

"They do," I said. "The line keeps them and binds them and they become the ships' libraries."

"That's intelligent," she said. "At least they are properly bound then. Now a book like that would have value."

I would walk along the quais when I had finished work or when I was trying to think something out. It was easier to think if I was walking and doing something or seeing people doing something that they understood. At the head of the Île de la Cité below the Pont Neuf where there was the statue of Henri Quatre, the island ended in a point like the sharp bow of a ship and there was a small park at the water's edge with fine chestnut trees, huge and spreading, and in the currents and back waters that the Seine made flowing past, there were excellent places to fish. You went down a stairway to the park and watched the fishermen there and under the great bridge. The good spots to fish changed with the height of the river and the fishermen used long, jointed, cane poles but fished with very fine leaders and light gear and quill floats and expertly baited the piece of water that they fished. They always caught some fish, and often they made excellent catches of the dace-like fish that were called *goujon*. They were delicious fried whole and I could eat a plateful. They were plump and sweet-fleshed with a finer flavor than fresh sardines even, and were not at all oily, and we ate them bones and all.

One of the best places to eat them was at an open-air restaurant built out over the river at Bas Meudon where we would go when we had money for a trip away from our quarter. It was called La Pêche Miraculeuse and had a splendid white wine that was a sort of Muscadet. It was a place out of a Maupassant story with the view over the river as Sisley had painted it. You did not have to go that far to eat *goujon*. You could get a very good *friture* on the Île St.-Louis.

I knew several of the men who fished the fruitful parts of the Seine between the Île St.-Louis and the Place du Verte Galente and sometimes, if the day was bright, I would buy a liter of wine and a piece of bread and some sausage and sit in the sun and read one of the books I had bought and watch the fishing.

Travel writers wrote about the men fishing in the Seine as though they were crazy and never caught anything; but it was serious and productive fishing. Most of the fishermen were men who had small pensions, which they did not know then would become worthless with inflation, or keen fishermen who fished on their days or half-days off from work. There was better fishing at Charenton, where the Marne came into the Seine, and on either side of Paris, but there was very good fishing in Paris itself. I did not fish because I did not have the tackle and I preferred to save my money to fish in Spain. Then too I never knew when I would be through working, nor when I would have to be away, and I did not want to become involved in the fishing which had its good times and its slack times. But I followed it closely and it was interesting and good to know about, and it always made me happy that there were men fishing in the city itself, having sound, serious fishing and taking a few *fritures* home to their families.

With the fishermen and the life on the river, the beautiful barges with their own life on board, the tugs with their smoke-stacks that folded back to pass under the bridges, pulling a tow of barges, the great elms on the stone banks of the river, the plane trees and in some places the poplars, I could never be lonely along the river. With so many trees in the city, you could see the spring coming each day until a night of warm wind would bring it suddenly in one morning. Sometimes the heavy cold rains would beat it back so that it would seem that it would never come and that you were losing a season out of your life. This was the only truly sad time in Paris because it was unnatural. You expected to be sad in the fall. Part of you died each year when the leaves fell from the trees and their branches were bare against the wind and the cold, wintry light. But you knew there would always be the spring, as you knew the river would flow again after it was frozen. When the cold rains kept on and killed the spring, it was as though a young person had died for no reason.

In those days, though, the spring always came finally but it was frightening that it had nearly failed.

A False Spring

WHEN spring came, even the false spring, there were no problems except where to be happiest. The only thing that could spoil a day was people and if you could keep from making engagements, each day had no limits. People were always the limiters of happiness except for the very few that were as good as spring itself.

In the spring mornings I would work early while my wife still slept. The windows were open wide and the cobbles of the street were drying after the rain. The sun was drying the wet faces of the houses that faced the window. The shops were still shuttered. The goatherd came up the street blowing his pipes and a woman who lived on the floor above us came out onto the sidewalk with a big pot. The goatherd chose one of the heavy-bagged, black milk-goats and milked her into the pot while his dog pushed the others onto the sidewalk. The goats looked around, turning their necks like sight-seers. The goatherd took the money from the woman and thanked her and went on up the street piping and the dog herded the goats on ahead, their horns bobbing. I went back to writing and the woman came up the stairs with the goat milk. She wore her felt-soled cleaning shoes and I only heard her breathing as she stopped on the stairs outside our door and then the shutting of her door. She was the only customer for goat milk in our building.

I decided to go down and buy a morning racing paper.

There was no quarter too poor to have at least one copy of a racing paper but you had to buy it early on a day like this. I found one in the rue Descartes at the corner of the Place Contrescarpe. The goats were going down the rue Descartes and I breathed the air in and walked back fast to climb the stairs and get my work done. I had been tempted to stay out and follow the goats down the early morning street. But before I started work again I looked at the paper. They were running at Enghien, the small, pretty and larcenous track that was the home of the outsider.

So that day after I had finished work we would go racing. Some money had come from the Toronto paper that I did newspaper work for and we wanted a long shot if we could find one. My wife had a horse one time at Auteuil named Chèvre d'Or that was a hundred and twenty to one and leading by twenty lengths when he fell at the last jump with enough savings on him to keep us six months. We tried never to think of that. We were ahead on that year until Chèvre d'Or.

"Do we have enough money to really bet, Tatie?" my wife asked.

"No. We'll just figure to spend what we take. Is there something else you'd rather spend it for?"

"Well," she said.

"I know. It's been terribly hard and I've been tight and mean about money."

"No," she said. "But—"

I knew how severe I had been and how bad things had been. The one who is doing his work and getting satisfaction from it is not the one the poverty bothers. I thought of bathtubs and showers and toilets that flushed as things that inferior people to us had or that you enjoyed when you made trips, which we often made. There was always the public bathhouse down at the foot of the street by the river. My wife had never complained once about these things any more than she cried about Chèvre d'Or when he fell. She had cried for the horse, I remembered, but not for the money. I had been stupid when she needed a grey lamb jacket and had loved it once she had bought it. I had been stupid about other things too. It was all part of the fight against poverty that you never win except by not spending. Especially if you buy pictures instead of clothes. But then we did not think ever of ourselves as poor. We did not accept it. We thought we were superior people and other people that we looked down on and rightly mistrusted were rich. It had never seemed strange to me to wear sweatshirts for underwear to keep warm. It only seemed odd to the rich. We ate well and cheaply and drank well and cheaply and slept well and warm together and loved each other.

"I think we ought to go," my wife said. "We haven't been for such a long time. We'll take a lunch and some wine. I'll make good sandwiches."

"We'll go on the train and it's cheap that way. But let's not go if you don't think we should. Anything we'd do today would be fun. It's a wonderful day."

"I think we should go."

"You wouldn't rather spend it some other way?"

"No," she said arrogantly. She had the lovely high cheekbones for arrogance. "Who are we anyway?"

So we went out by the train from the Gare du Nord through the dirtiest and saddest part of town and walked from the siding to the oasis of the track. It was early and we sat on my raincoat on the fresh cropped grass bank and had our lunch and drank from the wine bottle and looked at the old grandstand, the brown wooden betting booths, the green of the track, the darker green of the hurdles, and the brown shine of the water jumps and the whitewashed stone walls and white posts and rails, the paddock under the new leafed trees and the first horses being walked to the paddock. We drank more wine and studied the form in the paper and my wife lay down on the raincoat to sleep with the sun on her face. I went over and found someone I knew from the old days at San Siro in Milano. He gave me two horses.

"Mind, they're no investment. But don't let the price put you off."

We won the first with half of the money that we had to spend and he paid twelve to one, jumping beautifully, taking command on the far side of the course and coming in four lengths ahead. We saved half of the money and put it away and bet the other half on the second horse who broke ahead, led all the way over the hurdles and on the flat just lasted to the finish line with the favorite gaining on him with every jump and the two whips flailing.

We went to have a glass of champagne at the bar under the stand and wait for the prices to go up.

"My, but racing is very hard on people," my wife said. "Did you see that horse come up on him?"

"I can still feel it inside me."

"What will he pay?"

"The *cote* was eighteen to one. But they may have bet him at the last."

The horses came by, ours wet, with his nostrils working wide to breathe, the jockey patting him.

"Poor him," my wife said. "We just bet."

We watched them go on by and had another glass of champagne and then the winning price came up: 85. That meant he paid eighty-five francs for ten.

"They must have put a lot of money on at the end," I said.

But we had made plenty of money, big money for us, and now we had spring and money too. I thought that was all we needed. A day like that one, if you split the winnings one quarter for each to spend, left a half for racing capital. I kept the racing capital secret and apart from all other capital.

Another day later that year when we had come back from one of our voyages and had good luck at some track again we stopped at Pruniers on the way home, going in to sit at the bar after looking at all the clearly priced wonders in the window. We had oysters and *crabe Mexicaine* with glasses of Sancerre. We walked back through the Tuileries in the dark and stood and looked through the Arc du Carrousel up across the dark gardens with the lights of the Concorde behind the formal darkness and then the long rise of lights toward the Arc de Triomphe. Then we looked back toward the dark of the Louvre and I said, "Do you really think that the three arches are in line? These two and the Sermione in Milano?"

"I don't know, Tatie. They say so and they ought to know. Do you remember when we came out into the spring on the Italian side of the St. Bernard after the climb in the snow, and you and Chink and I walked down all day in the spring to Aosta?"

"Chink called it 'across the St. Bernard in street shoes.' Remember your shoes?"

"My poor shoes. Do you remember us having fruit cup at

Biffi's in the Galleria with Capri and fresh peaches and wild strawberries in a tall glass pitcher with ice?"

"That time was what made me wonder about the three arches."

"I remember the Sermione. It's like this arch."

"Do you remember the inn at Aigle where you and Chink sat in the garden that day and read while I fished?"

"Yes, Tatie."

I remembered the Rhône, narrow and grey and full of snow water and the two trout streams on either side, the Stockalper and the Rhône canal. The Stockalper was really clear that day and the Rhône canal was still murky.

"Do you remember when the horse-chestnut trees were in bloom and how I tried to remember a story that Jim Gamble, I think, had told me about a wisteria vine and I couldn't remember it?"

"Yes Tatie, and you and Chink always talking about how to make things true, writing them, and put them rightly and not describe. I remember everything. Sometimes he was right and sometimes you were right. I remember the lights and textures and the shapes you argued about."

Now we had come out of the gateway through the Louvre and crossed the street outside and were standing on the bridge leaning on the stone and looking down at the river.

"We all three argued about everything and always specific things and we made fun of each other. I remember everything we ever did and everything we ever said on the whole trip," Hadley said. "I do really. About everything. When you and Chink talked I was included. It wasn't like being a wife at Miss Stein's."

"I wish I could remember the story about the wisteria vine."

"It wasn't important. It was the vine that was important, Tatie."

"Do you remember I brought some wine from Aigle home to the chalet? They sold it to us at the inn. They said it should go with the trout. We brought it wrapped in copies of *La Gazette de Lausanne*, I think."

"The Sion wine was even better. Do you remember how Mrs. Gangeswisch cooked the trout *au bleu* when we got back to the chalet? They were such wonderful trout, Tatie, and we drank the Sion wine and ate out on the porch with the mountainside dropping off below and we could look across the lake and see the Dent du Midi with the snow half down it and the trees at the mouth of the Rhône where it flowed into the lake."

"We always miss Chink in the winter and the spring."

"Always. And I miss him now when it is gone."

Chink was a professional soldier and had gone out to Mons from Sandhurst. I had met him first in Italy and he had been my best friend and then our best friend for a long time. He spent his leaves with us then.

"He's going to try to get leave this next spring. He wrote last week from Cologne."

"I know. We should live in this time now and have every minute of it."

"We're watching the water now as it hits this buttress. Look what we can see when we look up the river."

We looked and there it all was: our river and our city and the island of our city.

"We're too lucky," she said. "I hope Chink will come. He takes care of us."

"He doesn't think so."

"Of course not."

"He thinks we explore together."

"We do. But it depends on what you explore."

We walked across the bridge and were on our own side of the river.

"Are you hungry again?" I said. "Us. Talking and walking."

"Of course, Tatie. Aren't you?"

"Let's go to a wonderful place and have a truly grand dinner."

"Where?"

"Michaud's?"

"That's perfect and it's so close."

So we walked up the rue des Saints-Pères to the corner of the rue Jacob stopping and looking in the windows at pictures and at furniture. We stood outside of Michaud's restaurant reading the posted menu. Michaud's was crowded and we waited for people to come out, watching the tables where people already had their coffee.

We were hungry again from walking and Michaud's was an exciting and expensive restaurant for us. It was where Joyce ate with his family then, he and his wife against the wall, Joyce peering at the menu through his thick glasses holding the menu up in one hand; Nora by him, a hearty but delicate eater; Giorgio thin, foppish, sleek-headed from the back; Lucia with heavy curly hair, a girl not quite yet grown; all of them talking Italian.

Standing there I wondered how much of what we had felt on the bridge was just hunger. I asked my wife and she said, "I don't know, Tatie. There are so many sorts of hunger. In the spring there are more. But that's gone now. Memory is hunger."

I was being stupid, and looking in the window and seeing two *tournedos* being served I knew I was hungry in a simple way.

"You said we were lucky today. Of course we were. But we had very good advice and information."

She laughed.

"I didn't mean about the racing. You're such a literal boy. I meant lucky other ways."

"I don't think Chink cares for racing," I said compounding my stupidity.

"No. He'd only care for it if he were riding."

"Don't you want to go racing any more?"

"Of course. And now we can go whenever we want again."

"But you really want to go?"

"Of course. You do, don't you?"

It was a wonderful meal at Michaud's after we got in; but when we had finished and there was no question of hunger any more the feeling that had been like hunger when we were on the bridge was still there when we caught the bus home. It was there when we came in the room and after we had gone to bed and made love in the dark, it was there. When I woke with the windows open and the moonlight on the roofs of the tall houses, it was there. I put my face away from the moonlight into the shadow but I could not sleep and lay awake thinking about it. We had both wakened twice in the night and my wife slept sweetly now with the moonlight on her face. I had to try to think it out and I was too stupid. Life had seemed so simple that morning when I had wakened and found the false spring and heard the pipes of the man with his herd of goats and gone out and bought the racing paper.

But Paris was a very old city and we were young and nothing was simple there, not even poverty, nor sudden money, nor the moonlight, nor right and wrong nor the breathing of someone who lay beside you in the moonlight.

The End of an Avocation

W<small>E WENT</small> racing together many more times that year and other years after I had worked in the early mornings, and Hadley enjoyed it and sometimes she loved it. But it was not the climbs in the high mountain meadows above the last forest, nor nights coming home to the chalet, nor was it climbing with Chink, our best friend, over a high pass into new country. It was not really racing either. It was gambling on horses. But we called it racing.

Racing never came between us, only people could do that; but for a long time it stayed close to us like a demanding friend. That was a generous way to think of it. I, the one who was so righteous about people and their destructiveness, tolerated this friend that was the falsest, most beautiful, most exciting, vicious, and demanding because she could be profitable. To make it profitable was more than a full-time job and I had no time for that. But I justified it to myself because I wrote it, even though in the end, when everything I had written was lost, there was only one racing story that survived, because it was out in the mails.

I was going to races alone more now and I was involved in them and getting too mixed up with them. I worked two tracks in their season when I could, Auteuil and Enghien. It took full-time work to try to handicap intelligently and you could make no money that way. That was just how it worked out on paper. You could buy a newspaper that gave you that.

You had to watch a jumping race from the top of the stands at Auteuil and it was a fast climb up to see what each horse did and see the horse that might have won and did not, and see why or maybe how he did not do what he could have done. You watched the prices and all the shifts of odds each time a horse you were following would start, and you had to know how he was working and finally get to know when the stable would try with him. He always might be beaten when he tried; but you should know by then what his chances were. It was hard work but at Auteuil it was beautiful to watch each day they raced when you could be there and see the honest races with the great horses, and you got to know the course as well as any place you had ever known. You knew many people finally, jockeys and trainers and owners and too many horses and too many things.

In principle I only bet when I had a horse to bet on but I sometimes found horses that nobody believed in except the men who trained and rode them that won race after race with me betting on them. I stopped finally because it took too much time, I was getting too involved and I knew too much about what went on at Enghien and at the flat racing tracks too.

When I stopped working on the races I was glad but it left an emptiness. By then I knew that everything good and bad left an emptiness when it stopped. But if it was bad, the emptiness filled up by itself. If it was good you could only fill it by finding something better. I put the racing capital back into the general funds and I felt relaxed and good.

The day I gave up racing I went over to the other side of the river and met my friend Mike Ward at the travel desk in the Guaranty Trust which was then at the corner of the rue des Italiens on the Boulevard des Italiens. I was depositing the racing capital but I did not tell that to anyone. I didn't put it in the checkbook though I still kept it in my head.

"Want to go to lunch?" I asked Mike.

"Sure, kid. Yeah I can do it. What's the matter? Aren't you going to the track?"

"No."

We had lunch at the square Louvois at a very good, plain bistro with a wonderful white wine. Across the square was the Bibliothèque Nationale.

"You never went to the track much, Mike," I said.

"No. Not for quite a long time."

"Why did you lay off it?"

"I don't know," Mike said. "Yes. Sure I do. Anything you have to bet on to get a kick isn't worth seeing."

"Don't you ever go out?"

"Sometimes to see a big race. One with great horses."

We spread paté on the good bistro bread and drank the white wine.

"Did you follow them a lot, Mike?"

"Oh yes."

"What do you see that's better?"

"Bicycle racing."

"Really?"

"You don't have to bet on it. You'll see."

"That track takes a lot of time."

"Too much time. Takes all your time. I don't like the people."

"I was very interested."

"Sure. You make out all right?"

"All right."

"Good thing to stop," Mike said.

"I've stopped."

"Hard to do. Listen kid, we'll go to the bike races sometime."

That was a new and fine thing that I knew little about. But we did not start it right away. That came later. It came to be a big part of our lives later when the first part of Paris was broken up.

But for a long time it was enough just to be back in our part of Paris and away from the track and to bet on our own life and work, and on the painters that you knew and not try to make your living gambling and call it by some other name. I have started many stories about bicycle racing but have never written one that is as good as the races are both on the indoor and outdoor tracks and on the roads. But I will get the Vélodrome d'Hiver with the smoky light of the afternoon and the high-banked wooden track and the whirring sound the tires made on the wood as the riders passed, the effort and the tactics as the riders climbed and plunged, each one a part of his machine; I will get the magic of the *demi-fond*, the noise of the motors with their rollers set out behind them that the *entraîneurs* rode, wearing their heavy crash helmets and leaning backward in their ponderous leather suits, to shelter the riders who followed them from the air resistance, the riders in their lighter crash helmets bent low over their handlebars their legs turning the huge gear sprockets and the small front wheels touching the roller behind the machine that gave them shelter to ride in, and the duels that were more exciting than anything, the *put-put*ing of the motorcycles and the riders elbow to elbow and wheel to wheel up and down and around at deadly speed until one man could not hold the pace and broke away and the solid wall of air that he had been sheltered against hit him.

There were so many kinds of racing. The straight sprints raced in heats or in match races where the two riders would balance for long seconds on their machines for the advantage of making the other rider take the lead and then the slow circling and the final plunge into the driving purity of speed. There were the programs of the team races of two hours, with a series of pure sprints in their heats to fill the afternoon, the lonely absolute speed events of one man racing an hour against the clock, the terribly dangerous and beautiful races of one hundred kilometers on the big banked wooden five-hundred-meter bowl of the Stade Buffalo, the outdoor stadium at Montrouge where they raced behind big motorcycles, Linart, the great Belgian champion that they called "the Sioux" for his profile, dropping his head to suck up cherry brandy from a rubber tube that connected with a hot water bottle under his racing shirt when he needed it toward the end as he increased his savage speed, and the championships of France behind big motors of the six-hundred-and-sixty-meter cement track of the Parc du Prince near Auteuil, the wickedest track of all where we saw that great rider Ganay fall and heard his skull crumple under the crash helmet as you crack an hard-boiled egg against a stone to peel it on a picnic. I must write the strange world of the six-day races and the marvels of the road-racing in the mountains. French is the only language it has ever been written in properly and the terms are all French and that is what makes it hard to write. Mike was right about it, there is no need to bet. But that comes at another time in Paris.

Hunger Was Good Discipline

You got very hungry when you did not eat enough in Paris because all the bakery shops had such good things in the windows and people ate outside at tables on the sidewalk so that you saw and smelled the food. When you had given up journalism and were writing nothing that anyone in America would buy, explaining at home that you were lunching out with someone, the best place to go was the Luxembourg gardens where you saw and smelled nothing to eat all the way from the Place de l'Observatoire to the rue de Vaugirard. There you could always go into the Luxembourg museum and all the paintings were sharpened and clearer and more beautiful if you were belly-empty, hollow-hungry. I learned to understand Cézanne much better and to see truly how he made landscapes when I was hungry. I used to wonder if he were hungry too when he painted; but I thought possibly it was only that he had forgotten to eat. It was one of those unsound but illuminating thoughts you have when you have been sleepless or hungry. Later I thought Cézanne was probably hungry in a different way.

After you came out of the Luxembourg you could walk down the narrow rue Férou to the Place St.-Sulpice and there were still no restaurants, only the quiet square with its benches and trees. There was a fountain with lions, and pigeons walked on the pavement and perched on the statues of the bishops.

There was the church and there were shops selling religious objects and vestments on the north side of the square.

From this square you could not go further toward the river without passing shops selling fruits, vegetables, wines, or bakery and pastry shops. But by choosing your way carefully you could work to your right around the grey and white stone church and reach the rue de l'Odéon and turn up to your right toward Sylvia Beach's bookshop and on your way you did not pass too many places where things to eat were sold. The rue de l'Odéon was bare of eating places until you reached the square where there were three restaurants.

By the time you reached 12 rue de l'Odéon your hunger was contained but all of your perceptions were heightened again. The photographs looked different and you saw books that you had never seen before.

"You're too thin, Hemingway," Sylvia would say. "Are you eating enough?"

"Sure."

"What did you eat for lunch?"

My stomach would turn over and I would say, "I'm going home for lunch now."

"At three o'clock?"

"I didn't know it was that late."

"Adrienne said the other night she wanted to have you and Hadley for dinner. We'd ask Fargue. You like Fargue, don't you? Or Larbaud. You like him. I know you like him. Or anyone you really like. Will you speak to Hadley?"

"I know she'd love to come."

"I'll send her a *pneu*. Don't you work so hard now that you don't eat properly."

"I won't."

"Get home now before it's too late for lunch."

"They'll save it."

"Don't eat cold food either. Eat a good hot lunch."

"Did I have any mail?"

"I don't think so. But let me look."

She looked and found a note and looked up happily and then opened a closed door in her desk.

"This came while I was out," she said. It was a letter and it felt as though it had money in it. "Wedderkop," Sylvia said.

"It must be from *Der Querschnitt*. Did you see Wedderkop?"

"No. But he was here with George. He'll see you. Don't worry. Perhaps he wanted to pay you first."

"It's six hundred francs. He says there will be more."

"I'm awfully glad you reminded me to look. Dear Mr. Awfully Nice."

"It's damned funny that Germany is the only place I can sell anything. To him and the *Frankfurter Zeitung*."

"Isn't it? But don't you worry ever. You can sell stories to Ford," she teased me.

"Thirty francs a page. Say one story every three months in *the transatlantic*. Story five pages long make one hundred and fifty francs a quarter. Six hundred francs a year."

"But, Hemingway, don't worry about what they bring now. The point is that you can write them."

"I know. I can write them. But nobody will buy them. There is no money coming in since I quit journalism."

"They will sell. Look. You have the money for one right there."

"I'm sorry, Sylvia. Forgive me for speaking about it."

"Forgive you for what? Always talk about it or about anything. Don't you know all writers ever talk about is their troubles? But promise me you won't worry and that you'll eat enough."

"I promise."

"Then get home now and have lunch."

Outside on the rue de l'Odéon I was disgusted with myself for having complained about things. I was doing what I did of my own free will and I was doing it stupidly. I should have bought a large piece of bread and eaten it instead of skipping a meal. I could taste the brown lovely crust. But it is dry in your mouth without something to drink. You God damn complainer. You dirty phony saint and martyr, I said to myself. You quit journalism of your own accord. You have credit and Sylvia would have loaned you money. She has plenty of times. Sure. And then the next thing you would be compromising on something else. Hunger is healthy and the pictures do look better when you are hungry. Eating is wonderful too and do you know where you are going to eat right now?

Lipp's is where you are going to eat and drink too.

It was a quick walk to Lipp's and every place I passed that my stomach noticed as quickly as my eyes or my nose made the walk an added pleasure. There were few people in the *brasserie* and when I sat down on the bench against the wall with the mirror in back and a table in front and the waiter asked if I wanted beer I asked for a *distingué*, the big glass mug that held a liter, and for potato salad.

The beer was very cold and wonderful to drink. The *pommes à l'huile* were firm and marinated and the olive oil delicious. I ground black pepper over the potatoes and moistened the bread in the olive oil. After the first heavy draft of beer I drank and ate very slowly. When the *pommes à l'huile* were gone I ordered another serving and a *cervelas*. This was a sausage like a heavy, wide frankfurter split in two and covered with a special mustard sauce.

I mopped up all the oil and all of the sauce with bread and drank the beer slowly until it began to lose its coldness and then I finished it and ordered a *demi* and watched it drawn. It seemed colder than the *distingué* and I drank half of it.

I had not been worrying, I thought. I knew the stories were good and someone would publish them finally at home. When I stopped doing newspaper work I was sure the stories were going to be published. But every one I sent out came back. What had made me so confident was Edward O'Brien's taking the "My Old Man" story for the *Best Short Stories* book and then dedicating the book for that year to me. Then I laughed and drank some more beer. The story had never been published in a magazine and he had broken all his rules to take it for the book. I laughed again and the waiter glanced at me. It was funny because, after all that, he had spelled the name wrong. It was one of two stories I had left when everything I had written was stolen in Hadley's suitcase that time at the Gare de Lyon when she was bringing the manuscripts down to me to Lausanne as a surprise, so I could work on them on our holidays in the mountains. She had put in the originals, the typescripts and the carbons, all in manila folders. The only reason I had the one story was that Lincoln Steffens had sent it out to some editor who sent it back. It was in the mail while everything else was stolen. The other story that I had was the one called "Up in Michigan" written before Miss Stein had come to our flat. I had never had it copied because she said it was *inaccrochable*. It had been in a drawer somewhere.

So after we had left Lausanne and gone down to Italy I showed the racing story to O'Brien, a gentle, shy man, pale, with pale blue eyes, and straight lanky hair he cut himself, who lived then as a boarder in a monastery up above Rapallo. It was a bad time and I did not think I could write any more then, and I showed the story to him as a curiosity, as you might show, stupidly, the binnacle of a ship you had lost in some incredible way, or as you might pick up your booted foot and make some joke about it if it had been amputated after a crash. Then, when he read the story, I saw he was hurt far more than I was. I had never seen anyone hurt by a thing other than death or unbearable suffering except Hadley when she told me about the things being gone. She had cried and cried and could not tell me. I told her that no matter what the dreadful thing was that had happened nothing could be that bad, and whatever it was, it was all right and not to worry. We would work it out. Then, finally, she told me. I was sure she could not have brought the carbons too and I hired someone to cover for me on my newspaper job. I was making good money then at journalism, and took the train for Paris. It was true all right and I remember what I did in the night after I let myself into the flat and found it was true. That was over now and Chink had taught me never to discuss casualties; so I told O'Brien not to feel so bad. It was probably good for me to lose early work and I told him all that stuff you feed the troops. I was going to start writing stories again

I said and, as I said it, only trying to lie so that he would not feel so bad, I knew that it was true.

Then I started to think in Lipp's about when I had first been able to write a story after losing everything. It was up in Cortina d'Ampezzo when I had come back to join Hadley there after the spring skiing which I had to interrupt to go on assignment to the Rhineland and the Ruhr. It was a very simple story called "Out of Season" and I had omitted the real end of it which was that the old man hanged himself. This was omitted on my new theory that you could omit anything if you knew that you omitted and the omitted part would strengthen the story and make people feel something more than they understood.

Well, I thought, now I have them so they do not understand them. There cannot be much doubt about that. There is most certainly no demand for them. But they will understand the same way that they always do in painting. It only takes time and it only needs confidence.

It is necessary to handle yourself better when you have to cut down on food so you will not get too much hunger-thinking. Hunger is good discipline and you learn from it. And as long as they do not understand it you are ahead of them. Oh sure, I thought, I'm so far ahead of them now that I can't afford to eat regularly. It would not be bad if they caught up a little.

I knew I must write a novel. But it seemed an impossible thing to do when I had been trying with great difficulty to write paragraphs that would be the distillation of what made a novel. It was necessary to write longer stories now as you would train for a longer race. When I had written a novel before, the one that had been lost in the bag stolen at the Gare de Lyon, I still had the lyric facility of boyhood that was as perishable and as deceptive as youth was. I knew it was probably a good thing that it was lost, but I knew too that I must write a novel. I would put it off though until I could not help doing it. I was damned if I would write one because it was what I should do if we were to eat regularly. When I had to write it, then it would be the only thing to do and there would be no choice. Let the pressure build. In the meantime I would write a long story about whatever I knew best.

By this time I had paid the check and gone out and turned to the right and crossed the rue de Rennes so that I would not go to the Deux-Magots for coffee and was walking up the rue Bonaparte on the shortest way home.

What did I know best that I had not written about and lost? What did I know about truly and care for the most? There was no choice at all. There was only the choice of streets to take you back fastest to where you worked. I went up Bonaparte to Guynemer, then to the rue d'Assas, up the rue Notre-Dame-des-Champs to the Closerie des Lilas.

I sat in a corner with the afternoon light coming in over my shoulder and wrote in the notebook. The waiter brought me a *café crème* and I drank half of it when it cooled and left it on the table while I wrote. When I stopped writing I did not want to leave the river where I could see the trout in the pool, its surface pushing and swelling smooth against the resistance of the log-driven piles of the bridge. The story was about coming back from the war but there was no mention of the war in it.

But in the morning the river would be there and I must

make it and the country and all that would happen. There were days ahead to be doing that each day. No other thing mattered. In my pocket was the money from Germany so there was no problem. When that was gone some other money would come in.

All I must do now was stay sound and good in my head until morning when I would start to work again.

Ford Madox Ford
and the Devil's Disciple

THE Closerie des Lilas was the nearest good café when we lived in the flat over the sawmill at 113 rue Notre-Dame-des-Champs, and it was one of the best cafés in Paris. It was warm inside in the winter and in the spring and fall it was very fine outside with the tables under the shade of the trees on the side where the statue of Marshal Ney was, and the square, regular tables under the big awnings along the boulevard. Two of the waiters were our good friends. People from the Dôme and the Rotonde never came to the Lilas. There was no one there they knew, and no one would have stared at them if they came. In those days many people went to the cafés at the corner of the Boulevard Montparnasse and the Boulevard Raspail to be seen publicly and in a way such places anticipated the columnists as the daily substitutes for immortality.

The Closerie des Lilas had once been a café where poets met more or less regularly and the last principal poet had been Paul Fort whom I had never read. But the only poet I ever saw there was Blaise Cendrars, with his broken boxer's face and his pinned-up empty sleeve, rolling a cigarette with his one good hand. He was a good companion until he drank too much and, at that time, when he was lying, he was more interesting than many men telling a story truly. But he was the only poet who came to the Lilas then and I only saw him there once. Most of the clients were elderly bearded men in well worn clothes who came with their wives or their mistresses and wore or did not wear thin red Legion of Honor ribbons in their lapels. We thought of them all hopefully as scientists or *savants* and they sat almost as long over an apéritif as the men in shabbier clothes who sat with their wives or mistresses over a *café crème* and wore the purple ribbon of the Palms of the Academy, which had nothing to do with the French Academy, and meant, we thought, that they were professors or instructors.

These people made it a comfortable café since they were all interested in each other and in their drinks or coffees, or infusions, and in the papers and periodicals which were fastened to rods, and no one was on exhibition.

There were other people too who lived in the quarter and came to the Lilas, and some of them wore Croix de Guerre ribbons in their lapels and others also had the yellow and green of the Médaille Militaire, and I watched how well they were overcoming the handicap of the loss of limbs, and saw the quality of their artificial eyes and the degree of skill with which their faces had been reconstructed. There was always an almost iridescent shiny cast about the considerably reconstructed face, rather like that of a well packed ski run, and we respected these clients more than we did the *savants* or the professors, although the latter might well have done their military service too without experiencing mutilation.

In those days we did not trust anyone who had not been in the war, but we did not completely trust anyone, and there was a strong feeling that Cendrars might well be a little less flashy about his vanished arm. I was glad he had been in the Lilas early in the afternoon before the regular clients had arrived.

On this evening I was sitting at a table outside of the Lilas watching the light change on the trees and the buildings and the passage of the great slow horses of the outer boulevards. The door of the café opened behind me and to my right, and a man came out and walked to my table.

"Oh here you are," he said.

It was Ford Madox Ford, as he called himself then, and he was breathing heavily through a heavy, stained mustache and holding himself as upright as an ambulatory, well clothed, up-ended hogshead.

"May I sit with you?" he asked, sitting down, and his eyes which were a washed-out blue under colorless lids and eyebrows looked out at the boulevard.

"I spent good years of my life that those beasts should be slaughtered humanely," he said.

"You told me," I said.

"I don't think so."

"I'm quite sure."

"Very odd. I've never told anyone in my life."

"Will you have a drink?"

The waiter stood there and Ford told him he would have a Chambéry Cassis. The waiter, who was tall and thin and bald on the top of his head with hair slicked over and who wore a heavy old-style dragoon mustache, repeated the order.

"No. Make it a *fine à l'eau*," Ford said.

"A *fine à l'eau* for Monsieur," the waiter confirmed the order.

I had always avoided looking at Ford when I could and I always held my breath when I was near him in a closed room, but this was the open air and the fallen leaves blew along the sidewalks from my side of the table past his, so I took a good look at him, repented, and looked across the boulevard. The light was changed again and I had missed the change. I took a drink to see if his coming had fouled it, but it still tasted good.

"You're very glum," he said.

"No."

"Yes you are. You need to get out more. I stopped by to ask you to the little evenings we're giving in that amusing Bal Musette near the Place Contrescarpe on the rue Cardinal Lemoine."

"I lived above it for two years before you came to Paris this last time."

"How odd. Are you sure?"

"Yes," I said. "I'm sure. The man who owned it had a taxi and when I had to get a plane he'd take me out to the field, and we'd stop at the zinc bar of the Bal and drink a glass of white wine in the dark before we'd start for the airfield."

"I've never cared for flying," Ford said. "You and your wife plan to come to the Bal Musette Saturday night. It's quite gay. I'll draw you a map so you can find it. I stumbled on it quite by chance."

"It's under 74 rue Cardinal Lemoine," I said. "I lived on the third floor."

"There's no number," Ford said. "But you'll be able to find it if you can find the Place Contrescarpe."

I took another long drink. The waiter had brought Ford's drink and Ford was correcting him. "It wasn't a brandy and soda," he said helpfully but severely. "I ordered a Chambéry vermouth and Cassis."

"It's all right, Jean," I said. "I'll take the *fine*. Bring Monsieur what he orders now."

"What I ordered," corrected Ford.

At that moment a rather gaunt man wearing a cape passed on the sidewalk. He was with a tall woman and he glanced at our table and then away and went on his way down the boulevard.

"Did you see me cut him?" Ford said. "*Did* you see me cut him?"

"No. Who did you cut?"

"Belloc," Ford said. "*Did* I cut him!"

"I didn't see it," I said. "Why did you cut him?"

"For every good reason in the world," Ford said. "*Did* I cut him though!"

He was thoroughly and completely happy. I had never seen Belloc and I did not believe he had seen us. He looked like a man who had been thinking of something and had glanced at the table almost automatically. I felt badly that Ford had been rude to him, as, being a young man who was commencing his education, I had a high regard for him as an older writer. This is not understandable now but in those days it was a common occurrence.

I thought it would have been pleasant if Belloc had stopped at the table and I might have met him. The afternoon had been spoiled by seeing Ford but I thought Belloc might have made it better.

"What are you drinking brandy for?" Ford asked me. "Don't you know it's fatal for a young writer to start drinking brandy?"

"I don't drink it very often," I said. I was trying to remember what Ezra Pound had told me about Ford, that I must never be rude to him, that I must remember that he only lied when he was very tired, that he was really a good writer and that he had been through very bad domestic troubles. I tried hard to think of these things but the heavy, wheezing, ignoble presence of Ford himself, only touching-distance away, made it difficult. But I tried.

"Tell me why one cuts people," I asked. Until then I had thought it was something only done in novels by Ouida. I had never been able to read a novel by Ouida, not even at some skiing place in Switzerland where reading matter had run out when the wet south wind had come and there were only the left-behind Tauchnitz editions of before the war. But I was sure, by some sixth sense, that people cut one another in her novels.

"A gentleman," Ford explained, "will always cut a cad."

I took a quick drink of brandy.

"Would he cut a bounder?" I asked.

"It would be impossible for a gentleman to know a bounder."

"Then you can only cut someone you have known on terms of equality?" I pursued.

"Naturally."

"How would one ever meet a cad?"

"You might not know it, or the fellow could have become a cad."

"What is a cad?" I asked. "Isn't he someone that one has to thrash within an inch of his life?"

"Not necessarily," Ford said.

"Is Ezra a gentleman?" I asked.

"Of course not," Ford said. "He's an American."

"Can't an American be a gentleman?"

"Perhaps John Quinn," Ford explained. "Certain of your ambassadors."

"Myron T. Herrick?"

"Possibly."

"Was Henry James a gentleman?"

"Very nearly."

"Are you a gentleman?"

"Naturally. I have held His Majesty's commission."

"It's very complicated," I said. "Am I a gentleman?"

"Absolutely not," Ford said.

"Then why are you drinking with me?"

"I'm drinking with you as a promising young writer. As a fellow writer in fact."

"Good of you," I said.

"You might be considered a gentleman in Italy," Ford said magnanimously.

"But I'm not a cad?"

"Of course not, dear boy. Who ever said such a thing?"

"I might become one," I said sadly. "Drinking brandy and all. That was what did for Lord Harry Hotspur in Trollope. Tell me, was Trollope a gentleman?"

"Of course not."

"You're sure?"

"There might be two opinions. But not in mine."

"Was Fielding? He was a judge."

"Technically perhaps."

"Marlowe?"

"Of course not."

"John Donne?"

"He was a parson."

"It's fascinating," I said.

"I'm glad you're interested," Ford said. "I'll have a brandy and water with you before I go."

After Ford left it was dark and I walked over to the *kiosque* and bought a *Paris-Sport Complet,* the final edition of the afternoon racing paper with the results at Auteuil, and the line on the next day's meeting at Enghien. The waiter Emile, who had replaced Jean on duty, came to the table to see the results of the last race at Auteuil. A great friend of mine who rarely came to the Lilas came over to the table and sat down, and just then as my friend was ordering a drink from Emile the gaunt man in the cape with the tall woman passed us on the sidewalk. His glance drifted toward the table and then away.

"That's Hilaire Belloc," I said to my friend. "Ford was here this afternoon and cut him dead."

"Don't be a silly ass," my friend said. "That's Alestair Crowley, the diabolist. He's supposed to be the wickedest man in the world."

"Sorry," I said.

Birth of a New School

THE blue-backed notebooks, the two pencils and the pencil sharpener (a pocket knife was too wasteful), the marble-topped tables, the smell of early morning, sweeping out and mopping, and luck were all you needed. For luck you carried a horse chestnut and a rabbit's foot in your right pocket. The fur had been worn off the rabbit's foot long ago and the bones and the sinews were polished by wear. The claws scratched in the lining of your pocket and you knew your luck was still there.

Some days it went so well that you could make the country so that you could walk into it through the timber to come out into the clearing and work up onto the high ground and see the hills beyond the arm of the lake. A pencil-lead might break off in the conical nose of the pencil sharpener and you would use the small blade of the pen knife to clear it or else sharpen the pencil carefully with the sharp blade and then slip your arm through the sweat-salted leather of your pack strap to lift the pack again, get the other arm through and feel the weight settle on your back and feel the pine needles under your moccasins as you started down for the lake.

Then you would hear someone say, "Hi, Hem. What are you trying to do? Write in a café?"

Your luck had run out and you shut the notebook. This was the worst thing that could happen. If you could keep your temper it would be better but I was not good at keeping mine then and said, "You rotten son of a bitch what are you doing in here off your filthy beat?"

"Don't be insulting just because you want to act like an eccentric."

"Take your dirty camping mouth out of here."

"It's a public café. I've just as much right here as you have."

"Why don't you go up to the Petite Chaumière where you belong?"

"Oh dear. Don't be so tiresome."

Now you could get out and hope it was an accidental visit and that the visitor had only come in by chance and there was not going to be an infestation. There were other good cafés to work in but they were a long walk away and this was my home café. It was bad to be driven out of the Closerie des Lilas. I had to make a stand or move. It was probably wiser to move but the anger started to come and I said, "Listen. A bitch like you has plenty of places to go. Why do you have to come here and louse a decent café?"

"I just came in to have a drink. What's wrong with that?"

"At home they'd serve you and then break the glass."

"Where's home? It sounds like a charming place."

He was sitting at the next table, a tall fat young man with spectacles. He had ordered a beer. I thought I would ignore him and see if I could write. So I ignored him and wrote two sentences.

"All I did was speak to you."

I went on and wrote another sentence. It dies hard when it is really going and you are into it.

"I suppose you've gotten so great nobody can speak to you."

I wrote another sentence that ended the paragraph and read it over. It was still all right and I wrote the first sentence of the next paragraph.

"You never think about anyone else or that they may have problems too."

I had heard complaining all my life. I found I could go on writing and that it was no worse than other noises, certainly better than Ezra learning to play the bassoon.

"Suppose you wanted to be a writer and felt it in every part of your body and it just wouldn't come."

I went on writing and I was beginning to have luck now as well as the other thing.

"Suppose once it had come like an irresistible torrent and then it left you mute and silent."

Better than mute and noisy, I thought, and went on writing. He was in full cry now and the unbelievable sentences were soothing as the noise of a plank being violated in the saw-mill.

"We went to Greece," I heard him say later. I had not heard him for some time except as noise. I was ahead now and I could leave it and go on tomorrow.

"You say you used it or you went there?"

"Don't be vulgar," he said. "Don't you want me to tell you the rest?"

"No," I said. I closed the notebook and put it in my pocket.

"Don't you care how it came out?"

"No."

"Don't you care about life and the suffering of a fellow human being?"

"Not you."

"You're beastly."

"Yes."

"I thought you could help me, Hem."

"I'd be glad to shoot you."

"Would you?"

"No. There's a law against it."

"I'd do anything for you."

"Would you?"

"Of course I would."

"Then keep the hell away from this café. Start with that."

I stood up and the waiter came over and I paid.

"Can I walk down to the sawmill with you, Hem?"

"No."

"Well I'll see you some other time."

"Not here."

"That's perfectly right," he said. "I promised."

"What are you writing?" I made a mistake and asked.

"I'm writing the best I can. Just as you do. But it's so terribly difficult."

"You shouldn't write if you can't write. What do you have to cry about it for? Go home. Get a job. Hang yourself. Only don't talk about it. You could never write."

"Why do you say that?"

"Did you ever hear yourself talk?"

"It's writing I'm talking about."

"Then shut up."

"You're just cruel," he said. "Everybody always said you were cruel and heartless and conceited. I always defended you. But not any more."

"Good."

"How can you be so cruel to a fellow human being?"

"I don't know," I said. "Look, if you can't write why don't you learn to write criticism?"

"Do you think I should?"

"It would be fine," I told him. "Then you can always write. You won't ever have to worry about it not coming nor being mute and silent. People will read it and respect it."

"Do you think I could be a good critic?"

"I don't know how good. But you could be a critic. There will always be people who will help you and you can help your own people."

"What do you mean my own people?"

"The ones you go around with."

"Oh them. They have their critics."

"You don't have to criticize books," I said. "There's pictures, plays, ballet, the cinema—"

"You make it sound fascinating, Hem. Thank you so much. It's so exciting. It's creative too."

"Creation's probably overrated. After all, God made the world in only six days and rested on the seventh."

"Of course there's nothing to prevent me doing creative writing too."

"Not a thing. Except you may set yourself impossibly high standards by your criticism."

"They'll be high. You can count on that."

"I'm sure they will be."

He was a critic already so I asked him if he would have a drink and he accepted.

"Hem," he said, and I knew he was a critic now since, in conversation, they put your name at the beginning of a sentence rather than at the end, "I have to tell you I find your work just a little too stark."

"Too bad," I said.

"Hem it's too stripped, too lean."

"Bad luck."

"Hem too stark, too stripped, too lean, too sinewy."

I felt the rabbit's foot in my pocket guiltily. "I'll try to fatten it up a little."

"Mind, I don't want it obese."

"Hal," I said, practicing speaking like a critic, "I'll avoid that as long as I can."

"Glad we see eye to eye," he said manfully.

"You'll remember about not coming here when I'm working?"

"Naturally, Hem. Of course. I'll have my own café now."

"You're very kind."

"I try to be," he said.

It would be interesting and instructive if the young man had turned out to be a famous critic but it did not turn out that way although I had high hopes for a while.

I did not think that he would come back the next day but I did not want to take chances and I decided to give the Closerie a day's rest. So the next morning I woke early, boiled the rubber nipples and the bottles, made the formula, finished the bottling, gave Mr. Bumby a bottle and worked on the dining-room table before anyone but he, F. Puss the cat, and I were awake. The two of them were quiet and good company and I worked better than I had ever done. In those days you did not really need anything, not even the rabbit's foot, but it was good to feel it in your pocket.

With Pascin at the Dôme

It was a lovely evening and I had worked hard all day and left the flat over the sawmill and walked out through the courtyard with the stacked lumber, closed the door, crossed the street and went into the back door of the bakery that fronted on the Boulevard Montparnasse and out through the good bread smells of the ovens and the shop to the street. The lights were on in the bakery and outside it was the end of the day and I walked in the early dusk up the street and stopped outside the terrace of the Nègre de Toulouse restaurant where our red and white checkered napkins were in the wooden napkin rings in the napkin rack waiting for us to come to dinner. I read the menu mimeographed in purple ink and saw that the *plat du jour* was cassoulet. It made me hungry to read the name.

Mr. Lavigne, the proprietor, asked me how my work had gone and I said it had gone very well. He said he had seen me working on the terrace of the Closerie des Lilas early in the morning but he had not spoken to me because I was so occupied.

"You had the air of a man alone in the jungle," he said.

"I am like a blind pig when I work."

"But were you not in the jungle, Monsieur?"

"In the bush," I said.

I went on up the street looking in the windows and happy with the spring evening and the people coming past. In the three principal cafés I saw people that I knew by sight and others that I knew to speak to. But there were always much nicer-looking people that I did not know that, in the evening with the lights just coming on, were hurrying to some place to drink together, to eat together and then to make love. The people in the principal cafés might do the same thing or they might just sit and drink and talk and love to be seen by others. The people that I liked and had not met went to the big cafés because they were lost in them and no one noticed them and they could be alone in them and be together. The big cafés were cheap then too, and all had good beer and the apéritifs cost reasonable prices that were clearly marked on the saucers that were served with them.

On this evening I was thinking these wholesome but not original thoughts and feeling extraordinarily virtuous because I had worked well and hard on a day when I had wanted to go out to the races very badly. But at this time I could not afford to go to the races, even though there was money to be made there if you worked at it. It was before the days of saliva tests and other methods of detecting artificially encouraged horses and doping was very extensively practiced. But handicapping beasts that are receiving stimulants, and detecting the symptoms in the paddock and acting on your perceptions, which sometimes bordered on the extrasensory, then backing them with money you cannot afford to lose, is not the way for a young man supporting a wife and child to get ahead in the full-time job of learning to write prose.

By any standards we were still very poor and I still made such small economies as saying that I had been asked out for lunch and then spending two hours walking in the Luxembourg gardens and coming back to describe the marvelous lunch to my wife. When you are twenty-five and are a natural heavyweight, missing a meal makes you very hungry. But it also sharpens all of your perceptions, and I found that many of the people I wrote about had very strong appetites and a great taste and desire for food, and most of them were looking forward to having a drink.

At the Nègre de Toulouse we drank the good Cahors wine from the quarter, the half, or the full carafe, usually diluting it about one-third with water. At home, over the sawmill, we had a Corsican wine that had great authority and a low price. It was a very Corsican wine and you could dilute it by half with water and still receive its message. In Paris, then, you could live very well on almost nothing and by skipping meals occasionally and never buying any new clothes, you could save and have luxuries.

Coming back from The Select now where I had sheered off at the sight of Harold Stearns who I knew would want to talk horses, those animals I was thinking of righteously and light-heartedly as the beasts that I had just foresworn. Full of my evening virtue I passed the collection of inmates at the Rotonde and, scorning vice and the collective instinct, crossed the boulevard to the Dôme. The Dôme was crowded too, but there were people there who had worked.

There were models who had worked and there were painters who had worked until the light was gone and there were writers who had finished a day's work for better or for worse, and there were drinkers and characters, some of whom I knew and some that were only decoration.

I went over and sat down at a table with Pascin and two

models who were sisters. Pascin had waved to me while I had stood on the sidewalk on the rue Delambre side wondering whether to stop and have a drink or not. Pascin was a very good painter and he was drunk; steady, purposefully drunk and making good sense. The two models were young and pretty. One was very dark, small, beautifully built with a falsely fragile depravity. The other was childlike and dull but very pretty in a perishable childish way. She was not as well built as her sister, but neither was anyone else that spring.

"The good and the bad sisters," Pascin said. "I have money. What will you drink?"

"*Une demi-blonde*," I said to the waiter.

"Have a whisky. I have money."

"I like beer."

"If you really liked beer, you'd be at Lipp's. I suppose you've been working."

"Yes."

"It goes?"

"I hope so."

"Good. I'm glad. And everything still tastes good?"

"Yes."

"How old are you?"

"Twenty-five."

"Do you want to bang her?" He looked toward the dark sister and smiled. "She needs it."

"You probably banged her enough today."

She smiled at me with her lips open. "He's wicked," she said. "But he's nice."

"You can take her over to the studio."

"Don't make piggishness," the blonde sister said.

"Who spoke to you?" Pascin asked her.

"Nobody. But I said it."

"Let's be comfortable," Pascin said. "The serious young writer and the friendly wise old painter and the two beautiful young girls with all of life before them."

We sat there and the girls sipped at their drinks and Pascin drank another *fine à l'eau* and I drank the beer; but no one was comfortable except Pascin. The dark girl was restless and she sat on display turning her profile and letting the light strike the concave planes of her face and showing me her breasts under the hold of the black sweater. Her hair was cropped short and was sleek and dark as an oriental's.

"You've posed all day," Pascin said to her. "Do you have to model that sweater now at the café?"

"It pleases me," she said.

"You look like a Javanese toy," he said.

"Not the eyes," she said. "It's more complicated than that."

"You look like a poor perverted little *poupée*."

"Perhaps," she said. "But alive. That's more than you."

"We'll see about that."

"Good," she said. "I like proofs."

"You didn't have any today?"

"Oh that," she said and turned to catch the last evening light on her face. "You were just excited about your work. He's in love with canvases," she said to me. "There's always some kind of dirtiness."

"You want me to paint you and pay you and bang you to keep my head clear, and be in love with you too," Pascin said. "You poor little doll."

"You like me, don't you, Monsieur?" she asked me.

"Very much."

"But you're too big," she said sadly.

"Everyone is the same size in bed."

"It's not true," her sister said. "And I'm tired of this talk."

"Look," Pascin said. "If you think I'm in love with canvases, I'll paint you tomorrow in water colors."

"When do we eat?" her sister asked. "And where?"

"Will you eat with us?" the dark girl asked.

"No. I go to eat with my *légitime*." That was what they said then. Now they say "my *régulière*."

"You have to go?"

"Have to and want to."

"Go on, then," Pascin said. "And don't fall in love with typewriting paper."

"If I do, I'll write with a pencil."

"Water colors tomorrow," he said. "All right, my children, I will drink another and then we eat where you wish."

"Chez Viking," the dark girl said.

"Me too," her sister urged.

"All right," Pascin agreed. "Good night, *jeune homme*. Sleep well."

"You too."

"They keep me awake," he said. "I never sleep."

"Sleep tonight."

"After Chez Les Vikings?" He grinned with his hat on the back of his head. He looked more like a Broadway character of the Nineties than the lovely painter that he was, and afterwards, when he had hanged himself, I liked to remember him as he was that night at the Dôme. They say the seeds of what we will do are in all of us, but it always seemed to me that in those who make jokes in life the seeds are covered with better soil and with a higher grade of manure.

Ezra Pound and His Bel Esprit

EZRA POUND was always a good friend and he was always doing things for people. The studio where he lived with his wife Dorothy on the rue Notre-Dame-des-Champs was as poor as Gertrude Stein's studio was rich. It had very good light and was heated by a stove and it had paintings by Japanese artists that Ezra knew. They were all noblemen where they came from and wore their hair cut long. Their hair glistened black and swung forward when they bowed and I was very impressed by them but I did not like their paintings. I did not understand them but they did not have any mystery, and when I understood them they meant nothing to me. I was sorry about this but there was nothing I could do about it.

Dorothy's paintings I liked very much and I thought Dorothy was very beautiful and built wonderfully. I also liked the head of Ezra by Gaudier-Brzeska and I liked all of the photographs of this sculptor's work that Ezra showed me and that were in Ezra's book about him. Ezra also liked Picabia's painting but I thought then that it was worthless. I also disliked Wyndham Lewis's painting which Ezra liked very much. He liked the works of his friends, which is beautiful as loyalty but can be disastrous as judgment. We never argued about these things because I kept my mouth shut about things I did not like. If a man liked his friends' painting or writing, I thought it was probably like those people who like their families, and it was not polite to criticize them. Sometimes you can go quite a long time before you criticize families, your own or those by marriage, but it is easier with bad painters because they do not do terrible things and make intimate harm as families can do. With bad painters all you need to do is not look at them. But even when you have learned not to look at families nor listen to them and have learned not to answer letters, families have many ways of being dangerous. Ezra was kinder and more Christian about people than I was. His own writing, when he would hit it right, was so perfect, and he was so sincere in his mistakes and so enamored of his errors, and so kind to people that I always thought of him as a sort of saint. He was also irascible but so perhaps have been many saints.

Ezra wanted me to teach him to box and it was while we were sparring late one afternoon in his studio that I first met Wyndham Lewis. Ezra had not been boxing very long and I was embarrassed at having him work in front of anyone he knew, and I tried to make him look as good as possible. But it was not very good because he knew how to fence and I was still working to make his left into his boxing hand and move his left foot forward always and bring his right foot up parallel with it. It was just basic moves. I was never able to teach him to throw a left hook and to teach him to shorten his right was something for the future.

Wyndham Lewis wore a wide black hat, like a character in the quarter, and was dressed like someone out of *La Bohème*. He had a face that reminded me of a frog, not a bullfrog but just any frog, and Paris was too big a puddle for him. At that time we believed that any writer or painter could wear any clothes he owned and there was no official uniform for the artist; but Lewis wore the uniform of a prewar artist. It was embarrassing to see him and he watched superciliously while I slipped Ezra's left leads or blocked them with an open right glove.

I wanted us to stop but Lewis insisted we go on, and I could see that, knowing nothing about what was going on, he was waiting, hoping to see Ezra hurt. Nothing happened. I never countered but kept Ezra moving after me sticking out his left hand and throwing a few right hands and then said we were through and washed down with a pitcher of water and toweled off and put on my sweatshirt.

We had a drink of something and I listened while Ezra and Lewis talked about people in London and Paris. I watched Lewis carefully without seeming to look at him, as you do when you are boxing, and I do not think I had ever seen a nastier-looking man. Some people show evil as a great race horse shows breeding. They have the dignity of a hard *chancre*. Lewis did not show evil; he just looked nasty.

Walking home I tried to think what he reminded me of and there were various things. They were all medical except toe-jam and that was a slang word. I tried to break his face down and describe it but I could only get the eyes. Under the black hat, when I had first seen them, the eyes had been those of an unsuccessful rapist.

"I met the nastiest man I've ever seen today," I told my wife.

"Tatie, don't tell me about him," she said. "Please don't tell me about him. We're just going to have dinner."

About a week afterwards I met Miss Stein and told her I'd met Wyndham Lewis and asked her if she had ever met him.

"I call him 'the Measuring Worm,'" she said. "He comes over from London and he sees a good picture and takes a pencil out of his pocket and you watch him measuring it on the pencil with his thumb. Sighting on it and measuring it and seeing exactly how it is done. Then he goes back to London and does it and it doesn't come out right. He's missed what it's all about."

So I thought of him as the Measuring Worm. It was a kinder and more Christian term than what I had thought about him myself. Later I tried to like him and to be friends with him as I did with nearly all of Ezra's friends when he explained them to me. But this was how he seemed to me on the first day I ever met him in Ezra's studio.

Ezra was the most generous writer I have ever known and the most disinterested. He helped poets, painters, sculptors and prose writers that he believed in and he would help anyone whether he believed in them or not if they were in trouble. He worried about everyone and in the time when I first knew him he was most worried about T. S. Eliot who, Ezra told me, had to work in a bank in London and so had insufficient time and bad hours to function as a poet.

Ezra founded something called Bel Esprit with Miss Natalie Barney who was a rich American woman and a patroness of the arts. Miss Barney had been a friend of Rémy de Gourmont who was before my time and she had a salon at her house on regular dates and a small Greek temple in her garden. Many American and French women with money enough had salons and I figured very early that they were excellent places for me to stay away from, but Miss Barney, I believe, was the only one that had a small Greek temple in her garden.

Ezra showed me the brochure for Bel Esprit and Miss Barney had allowed him to use the small Greek temple on the brochure. The idea of Bel Esprit was that we would all contribute a part of whatever we earned to provide a fund to get Mr. Eliot out of the bank so he would have money to write poetry. This seemed like a good idea to me and after we had got Mr. Eliot out of the bank Ezra figured we would go right straight along and fix up everybody.

I mixed things up a little by always referring to Eliot as Major Eliot pretending to confuse him with Major Douglas an economist about whose ideas Ezra was very enthusiastic. But Ezra understood that my heart was in the right place and that I was full of Bel Esprit even though it would annoy Ezra when I would solicit funds from my friends to get Major Eliot out of the bank and someone would say what was a Major doing in a bank anyway and if he had been axed by the military establishment did he not have a pension or at least some gratuity?

In such cases I would explain to my friends that this was all beside the point. Either you had Bel Esprit or you did not have it. If you had it you would subscribe to get the Major out of the bank. If you didn't it was too bad. Didn't they understand the significance of the small Greek temple? No? I thought so. Too bad, Mac. Keep your money. We wouldn't touch it.

As a member of Bel Esprit I campaigned energetically and my happiest dreams in those days were of seeing the Major stride out of the bank a free man. I cannot remember how Bel Esprit finally cracked up but I think it had something to do with the publication of *The Waste Land* which won the Major the Dial award and not long after a lady of title backed a review for Eliot called *The Criterion* and Ezra and I did not have to worry about him any more. The small Greek temple is, I believe, still in the garden. It was always a disappointment to me that we had not been able to get the Major out of the bank by Bel Esprit alone, as in my dreams I had pictured him as coming, perhaps, to live in the small Greek temple and that maybe I could go with Ezra when we would drop in to crown him with laurel. I knew where there was fine laurel that I could gather, riding out on my bicycle to get it, and I thought we could crown him any time he felt lonesome or any time Ezra had gone over the manuscript or the proofs of another big poem like *The Waste Land*. The whole thing turned out badly for me morally, as so many things have, because the money that I had earmarked for getting the Major out of the bank I took out to Enghien and bet on jumping horses that raced under the influence of stimulants. At two meetings the stimulated horses that I was backing outraced the unstimulated or insufficiently stimulated beasts except for one race in which our fancy had been overstimulated to such a point that before the start he threw his jockey and breaking away completed a full circuit of the steeplechase course jumping beautifully by himself the way one can sometimes jump in dreams. Caught up and remounted he started the race and figured honorably, as the French racing phrase has it, but was out of the money.

I would have been happier if the amount of the wager had gone to Bel Esprit which was no longer existent. But I comforted myself that with those wagers which had prospered I could have contributed much more to Bel Esprit than was my original intention.

A Strange Enough Ending

THE way it ended with Gertrude Stein was strange enough. We had become very good friends and I had done a number of practical things for her such as getting her long book started as a serial with Ford and helping type the manuscript and reading her proof and we were getting to be better friends than I could ever wish to be. There is not much future in men being friends with great women although it can be pleasant enough before it gets better or worse, and there is usually even less future with truly ambitious women writers. One time when I gave the excuse for not having stopped in at 27 rue de Fleurus for some time that I did not know whether Miss Stein would be at home, she said, "But Hemingway, you have the run of the place. Don't you know that? I mean it truly. Come in any time and the maidservant"—she used her name but I have forgotten it—"will look after you and you must make yourself at home until I come."

I did not abuse this but sometimes I would stop in and the maidservant would give me a drink and I would look at the pictures and if Miss Stein did not turn up I would thank the maidservant and leave a message and go away. Miss Stein and a companion were getting ready to go south in Miss Stein's car and on this day Miss Stein had asked me to come by in the forenoon to say good-by. She had asked us to come and visit, Hadley and I staying at an hotel, but Hadley and I had other plans and other places where we wanted to go.

Naturally you say nothing about this, but you can still hope to go and then it is impossible. I knew a little about the system of not visiting people. I had to learn it. Much later Picasso told me that he always promised the rich to come when they asked him because it made them so happy and then something would happen and he would be unable to appear. But that had nothing to do with Miss Stein and he said it about other people.

It was a lovely spring day and I walked down from the Place de l'Observatoire through the little Luxembourg. The horse-chestnut trees were in blossom and there were many children playing on the graveled walks with their nurses sitting on the benches, and I saw wood pigeons in the trees and heard others that I could not see.

The maidservant opened the door before I rang and told me to come in and to wait. Miss Stein would be down at any moment. It was before noon but the maidservant poured me a glass of *eau-de-vie*, put it in my hand and winked happily. The colorless alcohol felt good on my tongue and it was still in my mouth when I heard someone speaking to Miss Stein as I had never heard one person speak to another; never, anywhere, ever.

Then Miss Stein's voice came pleading and begging, saying, "Don't, pussy. Don't. Don't, please don't. I'll do anything, pussy, but please don't do it. Please don't. Please don't, pussy."

I swallowed the drink and put the glass down on the table and started for the door. The maidservant shook her finger at me and whispered, "Don't go. She'll be right down."

"I have to go," I said and tried not to hear any more as I left but it was still going on and the only way I could not hear it was to be gone. It was bad to hear and the answers were worse.

In the courtyard I said to the maidservant, "Please say I came to the courtyard and met you. That I could not wait because a friend is sick. Say *bon voyage* for me. I will write."

"*C'est entendu*, Monsieur. What a shame you cannot wait."

"Yes," I said. "What a shame."

That was the way it finished for me, stupidly enough, although I still did the small jobs, made the necessary appearances, brought people that were asked for and waited dismissal with most of the other men friends when that epoch came and the new friends moved in. It was sad to see new worthless pictures hung in with the great pictures but it made no difference any more. Not to me it didn't. She quarreled with nearly all of us that were fond of her except Juan Gris and she couldn't quarrel with him because he was dead. I am not sure that he would have cared because he was past caring and it showed in his paintings.

Finally she even quarreled with the new friends but none of us followed it any more. She got to look like a Roman emperor and that was fine if you liked your women to look like Roman emperors. But Picasso had painted her, and I could remember her when she looked like a woman from Friuli.

In the end everyone, or not quite everyone, made friends again in order not to be stuffy or righteous. I did too. But I could never make friends again truly, neither in my heart nor in my head. When you cannot make friends any more in your head is the worst. But it was more complicated than that.

The Man Who Was Marked for Death

THE afternoon I met Ernest Walsh, the poet, in Ezra's studio, he was with two girls in long mink coats and there was a long, shiny, hired car from Claridge's outside in the street with a uniformed chauffeur. The girls were blondes and they had crossed on the same ship with Walsh. The ship had arrived the day before and he had brought them with him to visit Ezra.

Ernest Walsh was dark, intense, faultlessly Irish, poetic and clearly marked for death as a character is marked for death in a motion picture. He was talking to Ezra and I talked with the girls who asked me if I had read Mr. Walsh's poems. I had not and one of them brought out a green-covered copy of Harriet Monroe's *Poetry, A Magazine of Verse* and showed me poems by Walsh in it.

"He gets twelve hundred dollars apiece," she said.

"For each poem," the other girl said.

My recollection was that I received twelve dollars a page, if that, from the same magazine. "He must be a very great poet," I said.

"It's more than Eddie Guest gets," the first girl told me.

"It's more than who's that other poet gets. You know."

"Kipling," her friend said.

"It's more than anybody gets ever," the first girl said.

"Are you staying in Paris very long?" I asked them.

"Well no. Not really. We're with a group of friends."

"We came over on this boat, you know. But there wasn't anyone on it really. Mr. Walsh was on it of course."

"Doesn't he play cards?" I asked.

She looked at me in a disappointed but understanding way.

"No. He doesn't have to. Not writing poetry the way he can write it."

"What ship are you going back on?"

"Well that depends. It depends on the boats and on a lot of things. Are you going back?"

"No. I'm getting by all right."

"This is sort of the poor quarter over here, isn't it?"

"Yes. But it's pretty good. I work the cafés and I'm out at the track."

"Can you go out to the track in those clothes?"

"No. This is my café outfit."

"It's kind of cute," one of the girls said. "I'd like to see some of that café life. Wouldn't you, dear?"

"I would," the other girl said. I wrote their names down in my address book and promised to call them at Claridge's. They were nice girls and I said good-by to them and to Walsh and to Ezra. Walsh was still talking to Ezra with great intensity.

"Don't forget," the taller one of the girls said.

"How could I?" I told her and shook hands with them both again.

The next I heard from Ezra about Walsh was that he had been bailed out of Claridge's by some lady admirers of poetry and of young poets who were marked for death, and the next thing, some time after that, was that he had financial backing from another source and was going to start a new magazine in the quarter as a co-editor.

At the time the *Dial*, an American literary magazine edited by Scofield Thayer, gave an annual award of, I believe, a thousand dollars for excellence in the practice of letters by a contributor. This was a huge sum for any straight writer to receive in those days, in addition to the prestige, and the award had gone to various people, all deserving, naturally. Two people, then, could live comfortably and well in Europe on five dollars a day and could travel.

This quarterly, of which Walsh was one of the editors, was alleged to be going to award a very substantial sum to the contributor whose work should be judged the best at the end of the first four issues.

If the news was passed around by gossip or rumor, or if it was a matter of personal confidence, cannot be said. Let us hope and believe always that it was completely honorable in every way. Certainly nothing could ever be said or imputed against Walsh's co-editor.

It was not long after I heard rumors of this alleged award that Walsh asked me to lunch one day at a restaurant that was the best and the most expensive in the Boulevard St.-Michel quarter and after the oysters, expensive flat faintly coppery *marennes*, not the familiar, deep, inexpensive *portugaises*, and a bottle of Pouilly-Fuissé, began to lead up to it delicately. He appeared to be conning me as he had conned the shills from the boat—if they were shills and if he had conned them, of course—and when he asked me if I would like another dozen of the flat oysters as he called them, I said I would like them very much. He did not bother to look marked for death with me and this was a relief. He knew I knew he had the con, not the kind you con with but the kind you died of then and how bad it was, and he did not bother to have to cough, and I was grateful for this at the table. I was wondering if he ate the flat oysters in the same way the whores in Kansas City, who were marked for death and practically everything else, always wished to swallow semen as a sovereign remedy against the con; but I did not ask him. I began my second dozen of the flat oysters, picking them from their bed of crushed ice on the silver plate, watching their unbelievably delicate brown edges react and cringe as I squeezed lemon juice on them and separated the holding muscle from the shell and lifted them to chew them carefully.

"Ezra's a great, great poet," Walsh said, looking at me with his own dark poet's eyes.

"Yes," I said. "And a fine man."

"Noble," Walsh said. "Truly noble." We ate and drank in silence as a tribute to Ezra's nobility. I missed Ezra and wished he were there. He could not afford *marennes* either.

"Joyce is great," Walsh said. "Great. Great."

"Great," I said. "And a good friend." We had become friends in his wonderful period after the finishing of *Ulysses* and before starting what was called for a long time *Work in Progress*. I thought of Joyce and remembered many things.

"I wish his eyes were better," Walsh said.

"So does he," I said.

"It is the tragedy of our time," Walsh told me.

"Everybody has something wrong with them," I said, trying to cheer up the lunch.

"You haven't." He gave me all his charm and more, and then he marked himself for death.

"You mean I am not marked for death?" I asked. I could not help it.

"No. You're marked for Life." He capitalized the word.

"Give me time," I said.

He wanted a good steak, rare, and I ordered two tournedos with sauce Béarnaise. I figured the butter would be good for him.

"What about a red wine?" he asked. The *sommelier* came and I ordered a Châteauneuf du Pape. I would walk it off afterwards along the quais. He could sleep it off, or do what he wanted to. I might take mine someplace, I thought.

It came as we finished the steak and french-fried potatoes and were two-thirds through the Châteauneuf du Pape which is not a luncheon wine.

"There's no use beating around the bush," he said. "You know you're to get the award, don't you?"

"Am I?" I said. "Why?"

"You're to get it," he said. He started to talk about my writing and I stopped listening. It made me feel sick for people to talk about my writing to my face, and I looked at him and his marked-for-death look and I thought, you con man conning me with your con. I've seen a battalion in the dust on the road, a third of them for death or worse and no special marks on them, the dust for all, and you and your marked for death look, you con man, making a living out of your death. Now you will con me. Con not, that thou be not conned. Death was not conning with him. It was coming all right.

"I don't think I deserve it, Ernest," I said, enjoying using my own name, that I hated, to him. "Besides, Ernest, it would not be ethical, Ernest."

"It's strange we have the same name, isn't it?"

"Yes, Ernest," I said. "It's a name we must both live up to. You see what I mean, don't you, Ernest?"

"Yes, Ernest," he said. He gave me complete, sad Irish understanding and the charm.

So I was always very nice to him and to his magazine and when he had his hemorrhages and left Paris asking me to see his magazine through the printers, who did not read English, I did that. I had seen one of the hemorrhages, it was very legitimate, and I knew that he would die all right, and it pleased me at that time, which was a difficult time in my life, to be extremely nice to him, as it pleased me to call him Ernest. Also, I liked and admired his co-editor. She had not promised me any award. She only wished to build a good magazine and pay her contributors well.

One day, much later, I met Joyce who was walking along the Boulevard St.-Germain after having been to a matinée alone. He liked to listen to the actors, although he could not see them. He asked me to have a drink with him and we went to the Deux-Magots and ordered dry sherry although you will always read that he drank only Swiss white wine.

"How about Walsh?" Joyce said.

"A such and such alive is a such and such dead," I said.

"Did he promise you that award?" Joyce asked.

"Yes."

"I thought so," Joyce said.

"Did he promise it to you?"

"Yes," Joyce said. After a time he asked, "Do you think he promised it to Pound?"

"I don't know."

"Best not to ask him," Joyce said. We left it at that. I told Joyce of my first meeting with him in Ezra's studio with the girls in the long fur coats and it made him happy to hear the story.

Evan Shipman at the Lilas

From the day I had found Sylvia Beach's library I had read all of Turgenev, what had been published in English of Gogol, the Constance Garnett translations of Tolstoi and the English translations of Chekov. In Toronto, before we had ever come to Paris, I had been told Katherine Mansfield was a good short-story writer, even a great short-story writer, but trying to read her after Chekov was like hearing the carefully artificial tales of a young old-maid compared to those of an articulate and knowing physician who was a good and simple writer. Mansfield was like near-beer. It was better to drink water. But Chekov was not water except for the clarity. There were some stories that seemed to be only journalism. But there were wonderful ones too.

In Dostoyevsky there were things believable and not to be believed, but some so true they changed you as you read them; frailty and madness, wickedness and saintliness, and the insanity of gambling were there to know as you knew the landscape and the roads in Turgenev, and the movement of troops, the terrain and the officers and the men and the fighting in Tolstoi. Tolstoi made the writing of Stephen Crane on the Civil War seem like the brilliant imagining of a sick boy who had never seen war but had only read the battles and chronicles and seen the Brady photographs that I had read and seen at my grandparents' house. Until I read the *Chartreuse de Parme* by Stendhal I had never read of war as it was except in Tolstoi, and the wonderful Waterloo account by Stendhal was an accidental piece in a book that had much dullness. To have come on all this new world of writing, with time to read in a city like Paris where there was a way of living well and working, no matter how poor you were, was like having a great treasure given to you. You could take your treasure with you when you traveled too, and in the mountains where we lived in Switzerland and Italy, until we found Schruns in the high valley in the Vorarlberg in Austria, there were always the books, so that you lived in the new world you had found, the snow and the forests and the glaciers and their winter problems and your high shelter in the Hotel Taube in the village in the day time, and at night you could live in the other wonderful world the Russian writers were giving you. At first there were the Russians; then there were all the others. But for a long time there were the Russians.

I remember asking Ezra once when we had walked home from playing tennis out on the Boulevard Arago, and he had asked me into his studio for a drink, what he really thought about Dostoyevsky.

"To tell you the truth, Hem," Ezra said, "I've never read the Rooshians."

It was a straight answer and Ezra had never given me any other kind verbally, but I felt very bad because here was the man I liked and trusted the most as a critic then, the man who believed in the *mot juste*—the one and only correct word to use—the man who had taught me to distrust adjectives as I would later learn to distrust certain people in certain situations; and I wanted his opinion on a man who almost never used the *mot juste* and yet had made his people come alive at times, as almost no one else did.

"Keep to the French," Ezra said. "You've plenty to learn there."

"I know it," I said. "I've plenty to learn everywhere."

Later after leaving Ezra's studio and walking along the street to the sawmill, looking down the high-sided street to the opening at the end where the bare trees showed and behind them the far façade of the Bal Bullier across the width of the Boulevard St.-Michel, I opened the gate and went in past the fresh-sawn lumber and left my racket in its press beside the stairs that led to the top floor of the pavillon. I called up the stairs but there was no one home.

"Madame has gone out and the *bonne* and the baby too," the wife of the sawmill owner told me. She was a difficult woman, over-plump, with brassy hair, and I thanked her.

"There was a young man to see you," she said, using the term *jeune homme* instead of monsieur. "He said he would be at the Lilas."

"Thank you very much," I said. "If Madame comes in, please tell her I am at the Lilas."

"She went out with friends," the wife said and gathering her purple dressing gown about her went on high heels into the doorway of her own *domaine* without closing the door.

I walked down the street between the high, stained and streaked white houses and turned to the right at the open, sunny end and went into the sun-striped dusk of the Lilas.

There was no one there I knew and I went outside onto the terrace and found Evan Shipman waiting. He was a fine poet and he knew and cared about horses, writing and painting. He rose and I saw him tall and pale and thin, his white shirt dirty and worn at the collar, his tie carefully knotted, his worn and wrinkled grey suit, his fingers stained darker than his hair, his nails dirty and his loving, deprecatory smile that he held tightly not to show his bad teeth.

"It's good to see you, Hem," he said.

"How are you, Evan?" I asked.

"A little down," he said. "I think I have the 'Mazeppa' licked though. Have you been going well?"

"I hope so," I said. "I was out playing tennis with Ezra when you came by."

"Is Ezra well?"

"Very."

"I'm so glad. Hem, you know I don't think that owner's wife where you live likes me. She wouldn't let me wait upstairs for you."

"I'll tell her," I said.

"Don't bother. I can always wait here. It's very pleasant in the sun now, isn't it?"

"It's fall now," I said. "I don't think you dress warmly enough."

"It's only cool in the evening," Evan said. "I'll wear my coat."

"Do you know where it is?"

"No. But it's somewhere safe."

"How do you know?"

"Because I left the poem in it." He laughed heartily holding his lips tightly over the teeth. "Have a whisky with me, please, Hem."

"All right."

"Jean," Evan got up and called the waiter. "Two whiskies please."

Jean brought the bottle and the glasses and two ten-franc

saucers with the syphon. He used no measuring glass and poured the whisky until the glasses were more than three-quarters full. Jean loved Evan who often went out and worked with him at his garden in Montrouge, out beyond the Porte d'Orléans, on Jean's day off.

"You mustn't exaggerate," Evan said to the tall old waiter.

"They are two whiskies, aren't they?" the waiter asked.

We added water and Evan said, "Take the first sip very carefully, Hem. Properly handled, they will hold us for some time."

"Are you taking any care of yourself?" I asked.

"Yes, truly, Hem. Let's talk about something else, should we?"

There was no one sitting on the terrace and the whisky was warming us both although I was better dressed for the fall than Evan as I wore a sweatshirt for underwear and then a shirt and a blue wool French sailor's sweater over the shirt.

"I've been wondering about Dostoyevsky," I said. "How can a man write so badly, so unbelievably badly, and make you feel so deeply?"

"It can't be the translation," Evan said. "She makes the Tolstoi come out well written."

"I know. I remember how many times I tried to read *War and Peace* until I got the Constance Garnett translation."

"They say it can be improved on," Evan said. "I'm sure it can although I don't know Russian. But we both know translations. But it comes out as a hell of a novel, the greatest I suppose, and you can read it over and over."

"I know," I said. "But you can't read Dostoyevsky over and over. I had *Crime and Punishment* on a trip when we ran out of books down at Schruns, and I couldn't read it again when we had nothing to read. I read the Austrian papers and studied German until we found some Trollope in Tauchnitz."

"God bless Tauchnitz," Evan said. The whisky had lost its burning quality and was now, when water was added, simply much too strong.

"Dostoyevsky was a shit, Hem," Evan went on. "He was best on shits and saints. He makes wonderful saints. It's a shame we can't reread him."

"I'm going to try *The Brothers* again. It was probably my fault."

"You can read some of it again. Most of it. But then it will start to make you angry, no matter how great it is."

"Well, we were lucky to have had it to read the first time and maybe there will be a better translation."

"But don't let it tempt you, Hem."

"I won't. I'm trying to do it so it will make it without you knowing it, and so the more you read it, the more there will be."

"Well I'm backing you in Jean's whisky," Evan said.

"He'll get in trouble doing that," I said.

"He's in trouble already," Evan said.

"How?"

"They're changing the management," Evan said. "The new owners want to have a different clientele that will spend some money and they are going to put in an American bar. The waiters are going to be in white jackets, Hem, and they have been ordered to be ready to shave off their mustaches."

"They can't do that to André and Jean."

"They shouldn't be able to, but they will."

"Jean has had a mustache all his life. That's a dragoon's mustache. He served in a cavalry regiment."

"He's going to have to cut it off."

I drank the last of the whisky.

"Another whisky, Monsieur?" Jean asked. "A whisky, Monsieur Shipman?" His heavy drooping mustache was a part of his thin, kind face, and the bald top of his head glistened under the strands of hair that were slicked across it.

"Don't do it, Jean," I said. "Don't take a chance."

"There is no chance," he said, softly to us. "There is much confusion. Many are leaving. *Entendu*, Messieurs," he said aloud. He went into the café and came out carrying the bottle of whisky, two large glasses, two ten-franc gold-rimmed saucers and a seltzer bottle.

"No, Jean," I said.

He put the glasses down on the saucers and filled them almost to the brim with whisky and took the remains of the bottle back into the café. Evan and I squirted a little seltzer into the glasses.

"It was a good thing Dostoyevsky didn't know Jean," Evan said. "He might have died of drink."

"What are we going to do with these?"

"Drink them," Evan said. "It's a protest. It's direct action."

On the following Monday when I went to the Lilas to work in the morning, André served me a *bovril*, which is a cup of beef extract and water. He was short and blond and where his stubby mustache had been, his lip was as bare as a priest's. He was wearing a white American barman's coat.

"And Jean?"

"He won't be in until tomorrow."

"How is he?"

"It took him longer to reconcile himself. He was in a heavy cavalry regiment throughout the war. He had the Croix de Guerre and the Médaille Militaire."

"I did not know he was so badly wounded."

"No. He was wounded of course but it was the other sort of Médaille Militaire he has. For gallantry."

"Tell him I asked for him."

"Of course," André said. "I hope it will not take him too long to reconcile himself."

"Please give him Mr. Shipman's greeting too."

"Mr. Shipman is with him," André said. "They are gardening together."

An Agent of Evil

THE last thing Ezra said to me before he left the rue Notre-Dame-des-Champs to go to Rapallo was, "Hem, I want you to keep this jar of opium and give it to Dunning only when he needs it."

It was a large cold-cream jar and when I unscrewed the top the content was dark and sticky and it had the smell of very raw opium. Ezra had bought it from an Indian chief, he said, on the avenue de l'Opéra near the Boulevard des Italiens and it had been very expensive. I thought it must have come from the old Hole in the Wall bar which was a hangout for deserters and for dope peddlers during and after the first war. The Hole in the Wall was a very narrow bar with a red-painted façade, little more than a passageway, on the rue des Italiens. At one time it had a rear exit into the sewers of Paris from which you were supposed to be able to reach the catacombs. Dunning was Ralph Cheever Dunning, a poet who smoked opium and forgot to eat. When he was smoking too much he could only drink milk and he wrote in *terza riruce* which endeared him to Ezra who also found fine qualities in his poetry. He lived in the same courtyard where Ezra had his studio and Ezra had called me in to help him when Dunning was dying a few weeks before Ezra was to leave Paris.

"Dunning is dying," Ezra's message said. "Please come at once."

Dunning looked like a skeleton as he lay on the mattress and he would certainly have eventually died of malnutrition but I finally convinced Ezra that few people ever died while speaking in well rounded phrases and that I had never known any man to die while speaking in *terza riruce* and that I doubted even if Dante could do it. Ezra said he was not talking in *terza riruce* and I said that perhaps it only sounded like *terza riruce* because I had been asleep when he had sent for me. Finally after a night with Dunning waiting for death to come, the matter was put in the hands of a physician and Dunning was taken to a private clinic to be disintoxicated. Ezra guaranteed his bills and enlisted the aid of I do not know which lovers of poetry on Dunning's behalf. Only the delivery of the opium in any true emergency was left to me. It was a sacred charge coming from Ezra and I only hoped I could live up to it and determine the state of a true emergency. It came when Ezra's concierge arrived one Sunday morning at the sawmill yard and shouted up to the open window where I was studying the racing form, *"Monsieur Dunning est monté sur le toit et refuse catégoriquement de descendre."*

Dunning having climbed to the roof of the studio and refusing categorically to come down seemed a valid emergency and I found the opium jar and walked up the street with the concierge who was a small and intense woman very excited by the situation.

"Monsieur has what is needed?" she asked me.

"Absolutely," I said. "There will be no difficulty."

"Monsieur Pound thinks of everything," she said. "He is kindness personified."

"He is indeed," I said. "And I miss him every day."

"Let us hope that Monsieur Dunning will be reasonable."

"I have what it takes," I assured her.

When we reached the courtyard where the studios were the concierge said, "He's come down."

"He must have known I was coming," I said.

I climbed the outside stairway that led to Dunning's place and knocked. He opened the door. He was gaunt and seemed unusually tall.

"Ezra asked me to bring you this," I said and handed him the jar. "He said you would know what it was."

He took the jar and looked at it. Then he threw it at me. It struck me on the chest or the shoulder and rolled down the stairs.

"You son of a bitch," he said. "You bastard."

"Ezra said you might need it," I said. He countered that by throwing a milk bottle.

"You are sure you don't need it?" I asked.

He threw another milk bottle. I retreated and he hit me with yet another milk bottle in the back. Then he shut the door.

I picked up the jar which was only slightly cracked and put it in my pocket.

"He did not seem to want the gift of Monsieur Pound," I said to the concierge.

"Perhaps he will be tranquil now," she said.

"Perhaps he has some of his own," I said.

"Poor Monsieur Dunning," she said.

The lovers of poetry that Ezra had organized rallied to Dunning's aid again eventually. My own intervention and that of the concierge had been unsuccessful. The jar of alleged opium which had been cracked I stored wrapped in waxed paper and carefully tied in one of an old pair of riding boots. When Evan Shipman and I were removing my personal effects from that apartment some years later the boots were still there but the jar was gone. I do not know why Dunning threw the milk bottles at me unless he remembered my lack of credulity the night of his first dying, or whether it was only an innate dislike of my personality. But I remember the happiness that the phrase *"Monsieur Dunning est monté sur le toit et refuse catégoriquement de descendre"* gave to Evan Shipman. He believed there was something symbolic about it. I would not know. Perhaps Dunning took me for an agent of evil or of the police. I only know that Ezra tried to be kind to Dunning as he was kind to so many people and I always hoped Dunning was as fine a poet as Ezra believed him to be. For a poet he threw a very accurate milk bottle. But Ezra, who was a very great poet, played a good game of tennis too. Evan Shipman, who was a very fine poet and who truly did not care if his poems were ever published, felt that it should remain a mystery.

"We need more true mystery in our lives, Hem," he once said to me. "The completely unambitious writer and the really good unpublished poem are the things we lack most at this time. There is, of course, the problem of sustenance."

Scott Fitzgerald

His talent was as natural as the pattern that was made by the dust on a butterfly's wings. At one time he understood it no more than the butterfly did and he did not know when it was brushed or marred. Later he became conscious of his damaged wings and of their construction and he learned to think and could not fly any more because the love of flight was gone and he could only remember when it had been effortless.

THE first time I ever met Scott Fitzgerald a very strange thing happened. Many strange things happened with Scott but this one I was never able to forget. He had come into the Dingo bar in the rue Delambre where I was sitting with some completely worthless characters, had introduced himself and introduced a tall, pleasant man who was with him as Dunc Chaplin, the famous pitcher. I had not followed Princeton baseball and had never heard of Dunc Chaplin but he was extraordinarily nice, unworried, relaxed and friendly and I much preferred him to Scott.

Scott was a man then who looked like a boy with a face between handsome and pretty. He had very fair wavy hair, a high forehead, excited and friendly eyes and a delicate long-lipped Irish mouth that, on a girl, would have been the mouth of a beauty. His chin was well built and he had good ears and a handsome, almost beautiful, unmarked nose. This should not have added up to a pretty face, but that came from the coloring, the very fair hair and the mouth. The mouth worried you until you knew him and then it worried you more.

I was very curious to see him and I had been working very hard all day and it seemed quite wonderful that here should be Scott Fitzgerald and the great Dunc Chaplin whom I had never heard of but who was now my friend. Scott did not stop talking and since I was embarrassed by what he said—

it was all about my writing and how great it was—I kept on looking at him closely and noticed instead of listening. We still went under the system, then, that praise to the face was open disgrace. Scott had ordered champagne and he and Dunc Chaplin and I drank it together with, I think, some of the worthless characters. I do not think that Dunc or I followed the speech very closely, for it was a speech and I kept on observing Scott. He was lightly built and did not look in awfully good shape, his face being faintly puffy. His Brooks Brothers clothes fitted him well and he wore a white shirt with a buttoned-down collar and a Guard's tie. I thought I ought to tell him about the tie, maybe, because they did have British in Paris and one might come into the Dingo—there were two there at the time—but then I thought the hell with it and I looked at him some more. It turned out later he had bought the tie in Rome.

I wasn't learning very much from looking at him now except that he had well shaped, capable-looking hands, not too small, and when he sat down on one of the bar stools I saw that he had very short legs. With normal legs he would have been perhaps two inches taller. We had finished the first bottle of champagne and started on the second and the speech was beginning to run down.

Both Dunc and I were beginning to feel even better than we had felt before the champagne and it was nice to have the speech ending. Until then I had felt that what a great writer I was had been carefully kept secret between myself and my wife and only those people we knew well enough to speak to. I was glad Scott had come to the same happy conclusion as to this possible greatness, but I was also glad he was beginning to run out of the speech. But after the speech came the question period. You could study him and neglect to follow the speech, but the questions were inescapable. Scott, I was to find, believed that the novelist could find out what he needed to know by direct questioning of his friends and acquaintances. The interrogation was direct.

"Ernest," he said. "You don't mind if I call you Ernest, do you?"

"Ask Dunc," I said.

"Don't be silly. This is serious. Tell me, did you and your wife sleep together before you were married?"

"I don't know."

"What do you mean you don't know?"

"I don't remember."

"But how can you not remember something of such importance?"

"I don't know," I said. "It is odd, isn't it?"

"It's worse than odd," Scott said. "You must be able to remember."

"I'm sorry. It's a pity, isn't it?"

"Don't talk like some limey," he said. "Try to be serious and remember."

"Nope," I said. "It's hopeless."

"You could make an honest effort to remember."

The speech comes pretty high, I thought. I wondered if he gave everyone the speech, but I didn't think so because I had watched him sweat while he was making it. The sweat had come out on his long, perfect Irish upper lip in tiny drops, and that was when I had looked down away from his face and checked on the length of his legs, drawn up as he sat on the bar stool. Now I looked back at his face again and it was then that the strange thing happened.

As he sat there at the bar holding the glass of champagne the skin seemed to tighten over his face until all the puffiness was gone and then it drew tighter until the face was like a death's head. The eyes sank and began to look dead and the lips were drawn tight and the color left the face so that it was the color of used candle wax. This was not my imagination. His face became a true death's head, or death mask, in front of my eyes.

"Scott," I said. "Are you all right?"

He did not answer and his face looked more drawn than ever.

"We'd better get him to a first aid station," I said to Dunc Chaplin.

"No. He's all right."

"He looks like he is dying."

"No. That's the way it takes him."

We got him into a taxi and I was very worried but Dunc said he was all right and not to worry about him. "He'll probably be all right by the time he gets home," he said.

He must have been because, when I met him at the Closerie des Lilas a few days later, I said that I was sorry the stuff had hit him that way and that maybe we had drunk it too fast while we were talking.

"What do you mean you are sorry? What stuff hit me what way? What are you talking about, Ernest?"

"I meant the other night at the Dingo."

"There was nothing wrong with me at the Dingo. I simply got tired of those absolutely bloody British you were with and went home."

"There weren't any British there when you were there. Only the bartender."

"Don't try to make a mystery of it. You know the ones I mean."

"Oh," I said. He had gone back to the Dingo later. Or he'd gone there another time. No, I remembered, there had been two British there. It was true. I remembered who they were. They had been there all right.

"Yes," I said. "Of course."

"That girl with the phony title who was so rude and that silly drunk with her. They said they were friends of yours."

"They are. And she *is* very rude sometimes."

"You see. There's no use to make mysteries simply because one has drunk a few glasses of wine. Why did you want to make the mysteries? It isn't the sort of thing I thought you would do."

"I don't know." I wanted to drop it. Then I thought of something. "Were they rude about your tie?" I asked.

"Why should they have been rude about my tie? I was wearing a plain black knitted tie with a white polo shirt."

I gave up then and he asked me why I liked this café and I told him about it in the old days and he began to try to like it too and we sat there, me liking it and he trying to like it, and he asked questions and told me about writers and publishers and agents and critics and George Horace Lorimer, and the gossip and economics of being a successful writer, and he was cynical and funny and very jolly and charming and endearing, even if you were careful about anyone becoming endearing. He spoke slightingly but without bitterness of everything he had written, and I knew his new book must be very good for him to speak, without bitterness, of the faults of past books. He wanted me to read the new book, *The Great Gatsby*, as soon as he could get his last and only copy back from someone he had loaned it to. To hear him talk of it, you would never know how very good it was, except that he had the shyness about it that all non-conceited writers have when they have done something very fine, and I hoped he would get the book quickly so that I might read it.

Scott told me that he had heard from Maxwell Perkins that the book was not selling well but that it had very fine reviews. I do not remember whether it was that day, or much later, that he showed me a review by Gilbert Seldes that could not have been better. It could only have been better if Gilbert Seldes had been better. Scott was puzzled and hurt that the book was not selling well but, as I said, he was not at all bitter then and he was both shy and happy about the book's quality.

On this day as we sat outside on the terrace of the Lilas and watched it get dusk and the people passing on the sidewalk and the grey light of the evening changing, there was no chemical change in him from the two whisky and sodas that we drank. I watched carefully for it, but it did not come and he asked no shameless questions, did nothing embarrassing, made no speeches, and acted as a normal, intelligent and charming person.

He told me that he and Zelda, his wife, had been compelled to abandon their small Renault motor car in Lyon because of bad weather and he asked me if I would go down to Lyon with him on the train to pick up the car and drive up with him to Paris. The Fitzgeralds had rented a furnished flat at 14 rue de Tilsitt not far from the Etoile. It was late spring now and I thought the country would be at its best and we could have an excellent trip. Scott seemed so nice and so reasonable, and I had watched him drink two good solid whiskies and nothing happened, and his charm and his seeming good sense made the other night at the Dingo seem like an unpleasant dream. So I said I would like to go down to Lyon with him and when did he want to leave.

We agreed to meet the next day and we then arranged to leave for Lyon on the express train that left in the morning. This train left at a convenient hour and was very fast. It made only one stop, as I recall, at Dijon. We planned to get into Lyon, have the car checked and in good shape, have an excellent dinner and get an early-morning start back towards Paris.

I was enthusiastic about the trip. I would have the company of an older and successful writer, and in the time we would have to talk in the car I would certainly learn much that it would be useful to know. It is strange now to remember thinking of Scott as an older writer, but at the time, since I had not yet read *The Great Gatsby*, I thought of him as a much older writer. I thought he wrote *Saturday Evening Post* stories that had been readable three years before but I never thought of him as a serious writer. He had told me at the Closerie des Lilas how he wrote what he thought were good stories, and which really were good stories for the *Post*, and then changed them for submission, knowing exactly how he must make the twists that made them into salable magazine stories. I had been shocked at this and I said I thought it was whoring. He said it was whoring but that he had to do it as he made his money from the magazines to have money ahead to write decent books. I said that I did not believe anyone could write any way except the very best he could write without destroying his talent. Since he wrote the real story first, he said, the destruction and changing of it that he did at the end did him no harm. I could not believe this and I wanted to argue him out of it but I needed a novel to back up my faith and to show him and convince him, and I had not yet written any such novel. Since I had started to break down all my writing and get rid of all facility and try to make instead of describe, writing had been wonderful to do. But it was very difficult, and I did not know how I would ever write anything as long as a novel. It often took me a full morning of work to write a paragraph.

My wife, Hadley, was happy for me to make the trip, though she did not take seriously the writing of Scott's that she had read. Her idea of a good writer was Henry James. But she thought it was a good idea for me to take a rest from work and make the trip, although we both wished that we had enough money to have a car and were making the trip ourselves. But that was something I never had any idea would happen. I had received an advance of two hundred dollars from Boni and Liveright for a first book of short stories to be published in America that fall, and I was selling stories to the *Frankfurter Zeitung* and to *Der Querschnitt* in Berlin and to *This Quarter* and *The Transatlantic Review* in Paris and we were living with great economy and not spending any money except for necessities in order to save money to go down to the *feria* at Pamplona in July and to Madrid and to the *feria* in Valencia afterwards.

On the morning we were to leave from the Gare de Lyon I arrived in plenty of time and waited outside the train gates for Scott. He was bringing the tickets. When it got close to the time for the train to leave and he had not arrived, I bought an entry ticket to the track and walked along the side of the train looking for him. I did not see him and as the long train was about to pull out I got aboard and walked through the train hoping only that he would be aboard. It was a long train and he was not on it. I explained the situation to the conductor, paid for a ticket, second class—there was no third—and asked the conductor for the name of the best hotel in Lyon. There was nothing to do but wire Scott from Dijon giving him the address of the hotel where I would wait for him in Lyon. He would not get it before he left, but his wife would be presumed to wire it on to him. I had never heard, then, of a grown man missing a train; but on this trip I was to learn many new things.

In those days I had a very bad, quick temper, but by the time we were through Montereau it had quieted down and I was not too angry to watch and enjoy the countryside and at noon I had a good lunch in the dining car and drank a bottle of St.-Émilion and thought that even if I had been a damned fool to accept an invitation for a trip that was to be paid for by someone else, and was spending money on it that we needed to go to Spain, it was a good lesson for me. I had never before accepted an invitation to go on any trip that was paid for, instead of the cost split, and in this one I had insisted that we split the cost of the hotels and meals. But now I did not know whether Fitzgerald would even show up. While I had been angry I had demoted him from Scott to Fitzgerald. Later I was delighted that I had used up the anger at the start and gotten it over with. It was not a trip designed for a man easy to anger.

In Lyon I learned that Scott left Paris for Lyon but had

left no word as to where he was staying. I confirmed my address there and the servant said she would let him know if he called. Madame was not well and was still sleeping. I called all the name hotels and left messages but could not locate Scott and then I went out to a café to have an apéritif and read the papers. At the café I met a man who ate fire for a living and also bent coins which he held in his toothless jaws with his thumb and forefinger. His gums were sore but firm to the eye as he exhibited them and he said it was not a bad *métier*. I asked him to have a drink and he was pleased. He had a fine dark face that glowed and shone when he ate the fire. He said there was no money in eating fire nor in feats of strength with fingers and jaws in Lyon. False fire-eaters had ruined the *métier* and would continue to ruin it wherever they were allowed to practice. He had been eating fire all evening, he said, and did not have enough money on him to eat anything else that night. I asked him to have another drink, to wash away the petrol taste of the fire-eating, and said we could have dinner together if he knew a good place that was cheap enough. He said he knew an excellent place.

We ate very cheaply in an Algerian restaurant and I liked the food and the Algerian wine. The fire-eater was a nice man and it was interesting to see him eat, as he could chew with his gums as well as most people can with their teeth. He asked me what I did to make a living and I told him that I was starting in as a writer. He asked what sort of writing and I told him stories. He said he knew many stories, some of them more horrible and incredible than anything that had ever been written. He could tell them to me and I would write them and then if they made any money I would give him whatever I thought fair. Better still we could go to North Africa together and he would take me to the country of the Blue Sultan where I could get stories such as no man had ever heard.

I asked him what sort of stories and he said battles, executions, tortures, violations, fearful customs, unbelievable practices, debaucheries; anything I needed. It was getting time for me to get back to the hotel and check on Scott again, so I paid for the meal and said we would certainly be running into each other again. He said he was working down toward Marseilles and I said sooner or later we would meet somewhere and it was a pleasure to have dined together. I left him straightening out bent coins and stacking them on the table and walked back to the hotel.

Lyon was not a very cheerful town at night. It was a big, heavy, solid-money town, probably fine if you had money and liked that sort of town. For years I had heard about the wonderful chicken in the restaurants there, but we had eaten mutton instead. The mutton had been excellent.

There was no word from Scott at the hotel and I went to bed in the unaccustomed luxury of the hotel and read a copy of the first volume of *A Sportsman's Sketches* by Turgenev that I had borrowed from Sylvia Beach's library. I had not been in the luxury of a big hotel for three years and I opened the windows wide and rolled up the pillows under my shoulders and head and was happy being with Turgenev in Russia until I was asleep while still reading. I was shaving in the morning getting ready to go out for breakfast when they called from the desk saying a gentleman was downstairs to see me.

"Ask him to come up, please," I said and went on shaving, listening to the town which had come heavily alive since early morning.

Scott did not come up and I met him down at the desk.

"I'm terribly sorry there was this mix-up," he said. "If I had only known what hotel you were going to it would have been simple."

"That's all right," I said. We were going to have a long ride and I was all for peace. "What train did you come down on?"

"One not long after the one you took. It was a very comfortable train and we might just as well have come down together."

"Have you had breakfast?"

"Not yet. I've been hunting all over the town for you."

"That's a shame," I said. "Didn't they tell you at home that I was here?"

"No. Zelda wasn't feeling well and I probably shouldn't have come. The whole trip has been disastrous so far."

"Let's get some breakfast and find the car and roll," I said.

"That's fine. Should we have breakfast here?"

"It would be quicker in a café."

"But we're sure to get a good breakfast here."

"All right."

It was a big American breakfast with ham and eggs and it was very good. But by the time we had ordered it, waited for it, eaten it, and waited to pay for it, close to an hour had been lost. It was not until the waiter came with the bill that Scott decided that we have the hotel make us a picnic lunch. I tried to argue him out of this as I was sure we could get a bottle of Mâcon in Mâcon and we could buy something to make sandwiches in a *charcuterie*. Or, if things were closed when we went through, there would be any number of restaurants where we could stop on our way. But he said I had told him that the chicken was wonderful in Lyon and that we should certainly take one with us. So the hotel made us a lunch that could not have cost us very much more than four or five times what it would have cost us if we had bought it ourselves.

Scott had obviously been drinking before I met him and, as he looked as though he needed a drink, I asked him if he did not want one in the bar before we set out. He told me he was not a morning drinker and asked if I was. I told him it depended entirely on how I felt and what I had to do and he said that if I felt that I needed a drink, he would keep me company so I would not have to drink alone. So we had a whisky and Perrier in the bar while we waited for the lunch and both felt much better.

I paid for the hotel room and the bar, although Scott wanted to pay for everything. Since the start of the trip I had felt a little complicated about it emotionally and I found I felt much better the more things I could pay for. I was using up the money we had saved for Spain, but I knew I had good credit with Sylvia Beach and could borrow and repay whatever I was wasting now.

At the garage where Scott had left the car, I was astonished to find that the small Renault had no top. The top had been damaged in unloading the car in Marseilles, or it had been damaged in Marseilles in some manner and Zelda had ordered it cut away and refused to have it replaced. His wife hated car tops, Scott told me, and without the top they had driven as far as Lyon where they were halted by the rain. The car was in fair shape otherwise and Scott paid the bill after disputing several charges for washing, greasing, and for adding two liters of oil. The garage man explained to me that the car needed new piston rings and had evidently been run without sufficient oil and water. He showed me how it had heated up and burned the paint off the motor. He said if I could persuade Monsieur to have a ring job done in Paris, the car, which was a good little car, would be able to give the service it was built for.

"Monsieur would not let me replace the top."

"No?"

"One has an obligation to a vehicle."

"One has."

"You gentlemen have no waterproofs?"

"No," I said. "I did not know about the top."

"Try and make Monsieur be serious," he said pleadingly. "At least about the vehicle."

"Ah," I said.

We were halted by rain about an hour north of Lyon.

In that day we were halted by rain possibly ten times. They were passing showers and some of them were longer than others. If we had waterproof coats it would have been pleasant enough to drive in that spring rain. As it was we sought the shelter of trees or halted at cafés alongside the road. We had a marvelous lunch from the hotel at Lyon, an excellent truffled roast chicken, delicious bread and white Mâcon wine and Scott was very happy when we drank the white Mâconnais at each of our stops. At Mâcon I had bought four more bottles of excellent wine which I uncorked as we needed them.

I am not sure Scott had ever drunk wine from a bottle before and it was exciting to him as though he were slumming or as a girl might be excited by going swimming for the first time without a bathing suit. But, by early afternoon, he had begun to worry about his health. He told me about two people who had died of congestion of the lungs recently. Both of them had died in Italy and he had been deeply impressed.

I told him that congestion of the lungs was an old-fashioned term for pneumonia, and he told me that I knew nothing about it and was absolutely wrong. Congestion of the lungs was a malady which was indigenous to Europe and I could not possibly know anything about it even if I had read my father's medical books, since they dealt with diseases that were strictly American. I said that my father had studied in Europe too. But Scott explained that congestion of the lungs had only appeared in Europe recently and that my father could not possibly have known anything about it. He also explained that diseases were different in different parts of America, and if my father had practiced medicine in New York instead of in the Middle West, he would have known an entirely different gamut of diseases. He used the word gamut.

I said that he had a good point in the prevalence of certain diseases in one part of the United States and their absence in others and cited the amount of leprosy in New Orleans and its low incidence, then, in Chicago. But I said that doctors had a system of exchange of knowledge and information among themselves and now that I remembered it after he had brought it up, I had read the authoritative article on congestion of the lungs in Europe in the *Journal of the American Medical Association* which traced its history back to Hippocrates himself.

This held him for a while and I urged him to take another drink of Mâcon, since a good white wine, moderately full-bodied but with a low alcoholic content, was almost a specific against the disease.

Scott cheered a little after this but he began to fail again shortly and asked me if we would make a big town before the onset of the fever and delirium by which, I had told him, the true congestion of the lungs, European, announced itself. I was now translating from an article which I had read in a French medical journal on the same malady while waiting at the American Hospital in Neuilly to have my throat cauterized, I told him. A word like cauterized had a comforting effect on Scott. But he wanted to know when we would make the town. I said if we pushed on we should make it in twenty-five minutes to an hour.

Scott then asked me if I were afraid to die and I said more at some times than at others.

It now began to rain really heavily and we took refuge in the next village at a café. I cannot remember all the details of that afternoon but when we were finally in a hotel at what must have been Châlon-sur-Saône, it was so late that the drug stores were closed. Scott had undressed and gone to bed as soon as we reached the hotel. He did not mind dying of congestion of the lungs, he said. It was only the question of who was to look after Zelda and young Scotty. I did not see very well how I could look after them since I was having a healthily rough time looking after my wife Hadley and young son Bumby, but I said I would do my best and Scott thanked me. I must see that Zelda did not drink and that Scotty should have an English governess.

We had sent our clothes to be dried and were in our pajamas. It was still raining outside but it was cheerful in the room with the electric light on. Scott was lying in bed to conserve his strength for his battle against the disease. I had taken his pulse, which was seventy-two, and had felt his forehead, which was cool. I had listened to his chest and had him breathe deeply, and his chest sounded all right.

"Look, Scott," I said. "You're perfectly O.K. If you want to do the best thing to keep from catching cold, just stay in bed and I'll order us each a lemonade and a whisky and you take an aspirin with yours and you'll feel fine and won't even get a cold in your head."

"Those old wives' remedies," Scott said.

"You haven't any temperature. How the hell are you going to have congestion of the lungs without a temperature?"

"Don't swear at me," Scott said. "How do you know I haven't a temperature?"

"Your pulse is normal and you haven't any fever to the touch."

"To the touch," Scott said bitterly. "If you're a real friend, get me a thermometer."

"I'm in pajamas."

"Send for one."

I rang for the waiter. He didn't come and I rang again and then went down the hallway to look for him. Scott was lying with his eyes closed, breathing slowly and carefully and, with his waxy color and his perfect features, he looked like a little dead crusader. I was getting tired of the literary life, if this was the literary life that I was leading, and already I missed not working and I felt the death loneliness that comes at the end of every day that is wasted in your life. I was very tired of Scott and of this silly comedy, but I found the waiter and gave him money to buy a thermometer and a tube of aspirin, and ordered two *citron pressés* and two double whiskies. I tried to order a bottle of whisky but they would only sell it by the drink.

Back in the room Scott was still lying as though on his tomb, sculpted as a momument to himself, his eyes closed and breathing with exemplary dignity.

Hearing me come in the room, he spoke. "Did you get the thermometer?"

I went over and put my hand on his forehead. It was not as cold as the tomb. But it was cool and not clammy.

"Nope," I said.

"I thought you'd brought it."

"I sent out for it."

"It's not the same thing."

"No. It isn't, is it?"

You could not be angry with Scott any more than you could be angry with someone who was crazy, but I was getting angry with myself for having become involved in the whole silliness. He did have a point though, and I knew it very well. Most drunkards in those days died of pneumonia, a disease which has now been almost eliminated. But it was hard to accept him as a drunkard, since he was affected by such small quantities of alcohol.

In Europe then we thought of wine as something as healthy and normal as food and also as a great giver of happiness and well being and delight. Drinking wine was not a snobbism nor a sign of sophistication nor a cult; it was as natural as eating and to me as necessary, and I would not have thought of eating a meal without drinking either wine or cider or beer. I loved all wines except sweet or sweetish wines and wines that were too heavy, and it had never occurred to me that sharing a few bottles of fairly light, dry, white Mâcon could cause chemical changes in Scott that would turn him into a fool. There had been the whisky and Perrier in the morning but, in my ignorance of alcoholics then, I could not imagine one whisky harming anyone who was driving in an open car in the rain. The alcohol should have been oxidized in a very short time.

While waiting for the waiter to bring the various things I sat and read a paper and finished one of the bottles of Mâcon that had been uncorked at the last stop. There are always some splendid crimes in the newspapers that you follow from day to day, when you live in France. These crimes read like continued stories and it is necessary to have read the opening chapters, since there are no summaries provided as there are in American serial stories and, anyway, no serial is as good in an American periodical unless you have read the all-important first chapter. When you are traveling through France the papers are disappointing because you miss the continuity of the different *crimes*, *affaires*, or *scandales*, and you miss much of the pleasure to be derived from reading about them in a café. Tonight I would have much preferred to be in a café where I might read the morning editions of the Paris papers and watch the people and drink something a little more authoritative than the Mâcon in preparation for dinner. But I was riding herd on Scott so I enjoyed myself where I was.

When the waiter arrived with the two glasses with the pressed lemon juice and ice, the whiskies, and the bottle of Perrier water, he told me that the pharmacy was closed and

he could not get a thermometer. He had borrowed some aspirin. I asked him to see if he could borrow a thermometer.
Scott opened his eyes and gave a baleful Irish look at the
waiter.

"Have you told him how serious it is?" he asked.

"I think he understands."

"Please try to make it clear."

I tried to make it clear and the waiter said, "I'll bring what
I can."

"Did you tip him enough to do any good? They only work
for tips."

"I didn't know that," I said. "I thought the hotel paid them
something on the side."

"I mean they will only do something for you for a substantial tip. Most of them are rotten clean through."

I thought of Evan Shipman and I thought of the waiter at
the Closerie des Lilas who had been forced to cut his mustache
when they made the American bar at the Closerie, and how
Evan had been working out at his garden in Montrouge long
before I had met Scott, and what good friends we all were
and had been for a long time at the Lilas and of all of the moves
that had been made and what they meant to all of us. I thought
of telling Scott about this whole problem of the Lilas, although
I had probably mentioned it to him before, but I knew he did
not care about waiters nor their problems nor their great kind-
nesses and affections. At that time Scott hated the French, and
since almost the only French he met with regularly were
waiters whom he did not understand, taxi-drivers, garage employees and landlords, he had many opportunities to insult
and abuse them.

He hated the Italians even more than the French and could

not talk about them calmly even when he was sober. The English he often hated but he sometimes tolerated them and occasionally looked up to them. I do not know how he felt about the Germans and the Austrians. I do not know whether he had ever met any then or any Swiss.

On this evening in the hotel I was delighted that he was being so calm. I had mixed the lemonade and whisky and given it to him with two aspirins and he had swallowed the aspirins without protest and with admirable calm and was sipping his drink. His eyes were open now and were looking far away. I was reading the *crime* in the inside of the paper and was quite happy, too happy it seemed.

"You're a cold one, aren't you?" Scott asked and looking at him I saw that I had been wrong in my prescription, if not in my diagnosis, and that the whisky was working against us.

"How do you mean, Scott?"

"You can sit there and read that dirty French rag of a paper and it doesn't mean a thing to you that I am dying."

"Do you want me to call a doctor?"

"No. I don't want a dirty French provincial doctor."

"What do you want?"

"I want my temperature taken. Then I want my clothes dried and for us to get on an express train for Paris and to go to the American hospital at Neuilly."

"Our clothes won't be dry until morning and there aren't any express trains," I said. "Why don't you rest and have some dinner in bed?"

"I want my temperature taken."

After this went on for a long time the waiter brought a thermometer.

"Is this the only one you could get?" I asked. Scott had shut his eyes when the waiter came in and he did look at least as far gone as Camille. I have never seen a man who lost the blood from his face so fast and I wondered where it went.

"It is the only one in the hotel," the waiter said and handed me the thermometer. It was a bath thermometer with a wooden back and enough metal to sink it in the bath. I took a quick gulp of the whisky sour and opened the window a moment to look out at the rain. When I turned Scott was watching me.

I shook the thermometer down professionally and said, "You're lucky it's not a rectal thermometer."

"Where does this kind go?"

"Under the arm," I told him and tucked it under my arm.

"Don't upset the temperature," Scott said. I shook the thermometer again with a single sharp downward twitch and unbuttoned his pajama jacket and put the instrument under his armpit while I felt his cool forehead and then took his pulse again. He stared straight ahead. The pulse was seventy-two. I kept the thermometer in for four minutes.

"I thought they only kept them in for one minute," Scott said.

"This is a big thermometer," I explained. "You multiply by the square of the size of the thermometer. It's a centigrade thermometer."

Finally I took the thermometer out and carried it over by the reading light.

"What is it?"

"Thirty-seven and six-tenths."

"What's normal?"

"That's normal."

"Are you sure?"

"Sure."

"Try it on yourself. I have to be sure."

I shook the thermometer down and opened my pajamas and put the thermometer in my armpit and held it there while I watched the time. Then I looked at it.

"What is it?" I studied it.

"Exactly the same."

"How do you feel?"

"Splendid," I said. I was trying to remember whether thirty-seven six was really normal or not. It did not matter, for the thermometer, unaffected, was steady at thirty.

Scott was a little suspicious so I asked if he wanted me to make another test.

"No," he said. "We can be happy it cleared up so quickly. I've always had great recuperative power."

"You're fine," I said. "But I think it would be just as well if you stayed in bed and had a light supper, and then we can start early in the morning." I had planned to buy us raincoats but I would have to borrow money from him for that and I did not want to start arguing about that now.

Scott did not want to stay in bed. He wanted to get up and get dressed and go downstairs and call Zelda so she would know he was all right.

"Why would she think you weren't all right?"

"This is the first night I have ever slept away from her since we were married and I have to talk to her. You can see what it means to us both, can't you?"

I could, but I could not see how he and Zelda could have slept together on the night just past; but it was nothing to argue about. Scott drank the whisky sour down very fast now and asked me to order another. I found the waiter and returned the thermometer and asked him how our clothes were coming along. He thought they might be dry in an hour or so. "Have the valet press them and that will dry them. It doesn't matter that they should be bone-dry."

The waiter brought the two drinks against catching cold and I sipped mine and urged Scott to sip his slowly. I was worried now he might catch cold and I could see by now that if he ever had anything as definitely bad as a cold he would probably have to be hospitalized. But the drink made him feel wonderful for a while and he was happy with the tragic implications of this being Zelda's and his first night of separation since their marriage. Finally he could not wait longer to call her and put on his dressing gown and went down to put the call through.

It would take some time for the call and shortly after he came up, the waiter appeared with two more double whisky sours. This was the most I had ever seen Scott drink until then, but they had no effect on him except to make him more animated and talkative, and he started to tell me the outline of his life with Zelda. He told me how he had first met her during the war and then lost her and won her back, and about their marriage and then about something tragic that had happened to them at St.-Raphael about a year ago. This first version that he told me of Zelda and a French naval aviator falling in love was truly a sad story and I believe it was a true story. Later he told me other versions of it as though trying them for use in a novel, but none was as sad as this first one and I always believed the first one, although any of them might have been true. They were better told each time; but they never hurt you the same way the first one did.

Scott was very articulate and told a story well. He did not have to spell the words nor attempt to punctuate and you did not have the feeling of reading an illiterate that his letters gave you before they had been corrected. I knew him for two years before he could spell my name; but then it was a long name to spell and perhaps it became harder to spell all of the time, and I give him great credit for spelling it correctly finally. He learned to spell more important things and he tried to think straight about many more.

On this night though he wanted me to know and understand and appreciate what it was that had happened at St.-Raphael and I saw it so clearly that I could see the single seater seaplane buzzing the diving raft and the color of the sea and the shape of the pontoons and the shadow that they cast and Zelda's tan and Scott's tan and the dark blonde and the light blond of their hair and the darkly tanned face of the boy that was in love with Zelda. I could not ask the question that was in my mind, how, if this story was true and it had all happened, could Scott have slept each night in the same bed with Zelda? But maybe that was what had made it sadder than any story anyone had ever told me then, and, too, maybe he did not remember, as he did not remember last night.

Our clothes came before the call did and we dressed and went downstairs to have dinner. Scott was a little unsteady now and he looked at people out of the side of his eyes with a certain belligerency. We had very good snails, with a carafe of Fleurie to start with and while we were about halfway through them Scott's call came. He was gone about an hour and I ate his snails finally, dipping up the butter, garlic and parsley sauce with broken bits of bread, and drank the carafe of Fleurie. When he came back I said I would get him some more snails but he said he did not want any. He wanted something simple. He did not want a steak, nor liver and bacon, nor an omelette. He would take chicken. We had eaten very good cold chicken at noon but this was still famous chicken country, so we had *poularde de Bresse* and a bottle of Montagny, a light, pleasant white wine of the neighborhood. Scott ate very little and sipped at one glass of the wine. He passed out at the table with his head on his hands. It was natural and there was no theater about it and it even looked as though he were careful not to spill nor break things. The waiter and I got him up to his room and laid him on the bed and I undressed him to his underwear, hung his clothes up, and then stripped the covers off the bed and spread them over him. I opened the window and saw it was clear outside and left the window open.

Downstairs I finished my dinner and thought about Scott. It was obvious he should not drink anything and I had not been taking good care of him. Anything that he drank seemed to stimulate him too much and then to poison him and I planned on the next day to cut all drinking to the minimum. I would tell him that we were getting back to Paris now and that I had to train in order to write. This was not true. My training was never to drink after dinner nor before I wrote nor while I was writing. I went upstairs and opened all the windows wide and undressed and was asleep almost as soon as I was in bed.

The next day we drove to Paris on a beautiful day up through the Côte d'Or with the air freshly washed and the hills and the fields and the vineyards all new, and Scott was very cheerful and happy and healthy and told me the plots of each and every one of Michael Arlen's books. Michael Arlen, he said, was the man you had to watch and he and I could both learn much from him. I said I could not read the books. He said I did not have to. He would tell me the plots and describe the characters. He gave me a sort of oral Ph.D. thesis on Michael Arlen.

I asked him if he had a good connection on the phone when he talked to Zelda and he said that it was not bad and that they had many things to talk about. At meals I ordered one bottle of the lightest wine I could locate and told Scott he would do me a great favor if he would not let me order any more as I had to train before I wrote and should not under any circumstances drink more than half a bottle. He co-operated wonderfully and when he saw me looking nervous toward the end of a single bottle, gave me some of his share.

When I had left him at his home and taken a taxi back to the sawmill, it was wonderful to see my wife and we went up to the Closerie des Lilas to have a drink. We were happy the way children are who have been separated and are together again and I told her about the trip.

"But didn't you have any fun or learn anything, Tatie?" she asked.

"I learned about Michael Arlen, if I would have listened, and I learned things I haven't sorted out."

"Isn't Scott happy at all?"

"Maybe."

"Poor man."

"I learned one thing."

"What?"

"Never to go on trips with anyone you do not love."

"Isn't that fine?"

"Yes. And we're going to Spain."

"Yes. Now it's less than six weeks before we go. And this year we won't let anyone spoil it, will we?"

"No. And after Pamplona we'll go to Madrid and to Valencia."

"M-m-m-m," she said softly, like a cat.

"Poor Scott," I said.

"Poor everybody," Hadley said. "Rich feathercats with no money."

"We're awfully lucky."

"We'll have to be good and hold it."

We both touched wood on the café table and the waiter came to see what it was we wanted. But what we wanted not he, nor anyone else, nor knocking on wood or on marble, as this café table-top was, could ever bring us. But we did not know it that night and we were very happy.

A day or two after the trip Scott brought his book over. It had a garish dust jacket and I remember being embarrassed by the violence, bad taste and slippery look of it. It looked the book jacket for a book of bad science fiction. Scott told me not to be put off by it, that it had to do with a billboard along a highway in Long Island that was important in the story. He said he had liked the jacket and now he didn't like it. I took it off to read the book.

When I had finished the book I knew that no matter what Scott did, nor how he behaved, I must know it was like a sickness and be of any help I could to him and try to be a good friend. He had many good, good friends, more than anyone I knew. But I enlisted as one more, whether I could be of any use to him or not. If he could write a book as fine as *The Great Gatsby* I was sure that he could write an even better one. I did not know Zelda yet, and so I did not know the terrible odds that were against him. But we were to find them out soon enough.

Hawks Do Not Share

Scott Fitzgerald invited us to have lunch with his wife Zelda and his little daughter at the furnished flat they had rented at 14 rue de Tilsitt. I cannot remember much about the flat except that it was gloomy and airless and that there was nothing in it that seemed to belong to them except Scott's first books bound in light blue leather with the titles in gold. Scott also showed us a large ledger with all of the stories he had published listed in it year after year with the prices he had received for them and also the amounts received for any motion picture sales, and the sales and royalties of his books. They were all noted as carefully as the log of a ship and Scott showed them to both of us with impersonal pride as though he were the curator of a museum. Scott was nervous and hospitable and he showed us his accounts of his earnings as though they had been the view. There was no view.

Zelda had a very bad hangover. They had been up on Montmartre the night before and had quarreled because Scott did not want to get drunk. He had decided, he told me, to work hard and not to drink and Zelda was treating him as though he were a kill-joy or a spoilsport. Those were the two words she used to him and there was recrimination and Zelda would say, "I did not. I did no such thing. It's not true, Scott." Later she would seem to recall something and would laugh happily.

On this day Zelda did not look her best. Her beautiful dark blonde hair had been ruined temporarily by a bad permanent she had gotten in Lyon, when the rain had made them abandon their car, and her eyes were tired and her face was too taut and drawn.

She was formally pleasant to Hadley and me but a big part of her seemed not to be present but to still be on the party she had come home from that morning. She and Scott both seemed to feel that Scott and I had enjoyed a great and wonderful time on the trip up from Lyon and she was jealous about it.

"When you two can go off and have such simply wonderful times together, it only seems fair that I should have just a little fun with our good friends here in Paris," she said to Scott.

Scott was being the perfect host and we ate a very bad lunch that the wine cheered a little but not much. The little girl was blonde, chubby-faced, well built, and very healthy looking and spoke English with a strong Cockney accent. Scott explained that she had an English nanny because he wanted her to speak like Lady Diana Manners when she grew up.

Zelda had hawk's eyes and a thin mouth and deep-south manners and accent. Watching her face you could see her mind leave the table and go to the night's party and return with her eyes blank as a cat's and then pleased, and the pleasure would show along the thin line of her lips and then be gone. Scott was being the good cheerful host and Zelda looked at him and she smiled happily with her eyes and her mouth too as he drank the wine. I learned to know that smile very well. It meant she knew Scott would not be able to write.

Zelda was jealous of Scott's work and as we got to know them, this fell into a regular pattern. Scott would resolve not to go on all-night drinking parties and to get some exercise each day and work regularly. He would start to work and as soon as he was working well Zelda would begin complaining about how bored she was and get him off on another drunken party. They would quarrel and then make up and he would sweat out the alcohol on long walks with me, and make up his mind that this time he would really work, and would start off well. Then it would start all over again.

Scott was very much in love with Zelda and he was very jealous of her. He told me many times on our walks of how she had fallen in love with the French navy pilot. But she had never made him really jealous with another man since. This spring she was making him jealous with other women and on the Montmartre parties he was afraid to pass out and he was afraid to have her pass out. Becoming unconscious when they drank had always been their great defense. They went to sleep on drinking an amount of liquor or champagne that would have little effect on a person accustomed to drinking, and they would go to sleep like children. I have seen them become unconscious not as though they were drunk but as though they had been anesthetized and their friends, or sometimes a taxi-driver, would get them to bed, and when they woke they would be fresh and happy, not having taken enough alcohol to damage their bodies before it made them unconscious.

Now they had lost this natural defense. At this time Zelda could drink more than Scott could and Scott was afraid for her to pass out in the company they kept that spring and the places they went to. Scott did not like the places nor the people and he had to drink more than he could drink and be in any control of himself, to stand the people and the places, and then he began to have to drink to keep awake after he would usually have passed out. Finally he had few intervals of work at all.

He was always trying to work. Each day he would try and fail. He laid the failure to Paris, the town best organized for a writer to write in that there is, and he thought always that there would be someplace where he and Zelda could have a good life together again. He thought of the Riviera, as it was then before it had all been built up, with the lovely stretches of blue sea and the sand beaches and the stretches of pine woods and the mountains of the Esterel going out into the sea. He remembered it as it was when he and Zelda had first found it before people went there for the summer.

Scott told me about the Riviera and how my wife and I must come there the next summer and how we would go there and how he would find a place for us that was not expensive and we would both work hard every day and swim and lie on the beach and be brown and only have a single apéritif before lunch and one before dinner. Zelda would be happy there, he said. She loved to swim and was a beautiful diver and she was happy with that life and would want him to work and everything would be disciplined. He and Zelda and their daughter were going to go there that summer.

I was trying to get him to write his stories as well as he could and not trick them to conform to any formula, as he had explained that he did.

"You've written a fine novel now," I told him. "And you mustn't write slop."

"The novel isn't selling," he said. "I must write stories and they have to be stories that will sell."

"Write the best story that you can and write it as straight as you can."

"I'm going to," he said.

But the way things were going, he was lucky to get any work done at all. Zelda did not encourage the people who were chasing her and she had nothing to do with them, she said. But it amused her and it made Scott jealous and he had to go with her to the places. It destroyed his work, and she was more jealous of his work than anything.

All that late spring and early summer Scott fought to work but he could only work in snatches. When I saw him he was always cheerful, sometimes desperately cheerful, and he made good jokes and was a good companion. When he had very bad times, I listened to him about them and tried to make him know that if he could hold onto himself he would write as he was made to write, and that only death was irrevocable. He would make fun of himself then, and as long as he could do that I thought that he was safe. Through all of this he wrote one good story, "The Rich Boy," and I was sure that he could write better than that as he did later.

During the summer we were in Spain and I started the first draft of a novel and finished it back in Paris in September. Scott and Zelda had been at Cap d'Antibes, and that fall when I saw him in Paris he was very changed. He had not done any sobering up on the Riviera and he was drunk now in the day time as well as nights. It did not make any difference any more to him that anyone was working and he would come to 113 rue Notre-Dame-des-Champs any time he was drunk either in the day time or at night. He had begun to be very rude to his inferiors or anyone he considered his inferior.

One time he came in through the sawmill gate with his small daughter—it was the English nurse's day off and Scott was caring for the child—and at the foot of the stairs she told him she needed to go to the bathroom. Scott started to undress her and the proprietor, who lived on the floor below us, came in and said, "Monsieur, there is a *cabinet de toilette* just ahead of you to the left of the stairs."

"Yes, and I'll put your head in it too, if you're not careful," Scott told him.

He was very difficult all that fall but he had begun to work on a novel when he was sober. I saw him rarely when he was sober, but when he was sober he was always pleasant and he still made jokes and sometimes he would still make jokes about himself. But when he was drunk he would usually come to find me and, drunk, he took almost as much pleasure interfering with my work as Zelda did interfering with his. This continued for years but, for years too, I had no more loyal friend than Scott when he was sober.

That fall of 1925 he was upset because I would not show him the manuscript of the first draft of *The Sun Also Rises.* I explained to him that it would mean nothing until I had gone over it and rewritten it and that I did not want to discuss it or show it to anyone first. We were going down to Schruns in the Vorarlberg in Austria as soon as the first snowfall there.

I rewrote the first half of the manuscript there, finished it in January, I think. I took it to New York and showed it to Max Perkins of Scribners and then went back to Schruns and finished rewriting the book. Scott did not see it until after the completed rewritten and cut manuscript had been sent to Scribners at the end of April. I remembered joking with him about it and him being worried and anxious to help as always once a thing was done. But I did not want his help while I was rewriting.

While we were living in the Vorarlberg and I was finishing rewriting the novel, Scott and his wife and child had left Paris for a watering place in the lower Pyrénées. Zelda had been ill with that familiar intestinal complaint that too much champagne produces and which was then diagnosed as colitis. Scott was not drinking, and starting to work and he wanted us to come to Juan-les-Pins in June. They would find an inexpensive villa for us and this time he would not drink and it would be like the old good days and we would swim and be healthy and brown and have one apéritif before lunch and one before dinner. Zelda was well again and they were both fine and his novel was going wonderfully. He had money coming in from a dramatization of *The Great Gatsby* which was running well and it would sell to the movies and he had no worries. Zelda was really fine and everything was going to be disciplined.

I had been down in Madrid in May working by myself and I came by train from Bayonne to Juan-les-Pins third class and quite hungry because I had run out of money stupidly and had eaten last in Hendaye at the French-Spanish frontier. It was a nice villa and Scott had a very fine house not far away and I was very happy to see my wife who had the villa running beautifully, and our friends, and the single apéritif before lunch was very good and we had several more. That night there was a party to welcome us at the Casino, just a small party, the MacLeishes, the Murphys, the Fitzgeralds and we who were living at the villa. No one drank anything stronger than champagne and it was very gay and obviously a splendid place to write. There was going to be everything that a man needed to write except to be alone.

Zelda was very beautiful and was tanned a lovely gold color and her hair was a beautiful dark gold and she was very friendly. Her hawk's eyes were clear and calm. I knew everything was all right and was going to turn out well in the end when she leaned forward and said to me, telling me her great secret, "Ernest, don't you think Al Jolson is greater than Jesus?"

Nobody thought anything of it at the time. It was only Zelda's secret that she shared with me, as a hawk might share something with a man. But hawks do not share. Scott did not write anything any more that was good until after he knew that she was insane.

A Matter of Measurements

Much later, in the time after Zelda had what was then called her first nervous breakdown and we happened to be in Paris at the same time, Scott asked me to have lunch with him at Michaud's restaurant on the corner of the rue Jacob and the rue des Saints-Pères. He said he had something very important to ask me that meant more than anything in the world to him and that I must answer absolutely truly. I said that I would do the best that I could. When he would ask me to tell him something absolutely truly, which is very difficult to do, and I would try it, what I said would make him angry, often not when I said it but afterwards, and sometimes long afterwards when he had brooded on it. My words would become something that would have to be destroyed and sometimes, if possible, me with them.

He drank wine at the lunch but it did not affect him and he had not prepared for the lunch by drinking before it. We talked about our work and about people and he asked me about people that we had not seen lately. I knew that he was writing something good and that he was having great trouble with it for many reasons but that was not what he wanted to talk about. I kept waiting for it to come, the thing that I had to tell the absolute truth about; but he would not bring it up until the end of the meal, as though we were having a business lunch.

Finally when we were eating the cherry tart and had a last

carafe of wine he said, "You know I never slept with anyone except Zelda."

"No, I didn't."

"I thought I had told you."

"No. You told me a lot of things but not that."

"That is what I have to ask you about."

"Good. Go on."

"Zelda said that the way I was built I could never make any woman happy and that was what upset her originally. She said it was a matter of measurements. I have never felt the same since she said that and I have to know truly."

"Come out to the office," I said.

"Where is the office?"

"Le water," I said.

We came back into the room and sat down at the table.

"You're perfectly fine," I said. "You are O.K. There's nothing wrong with you. You look at yourself from above and you look foreshortened. Go over to the Louvre and look at the people in the statues and then go home and look at yourself in the mirror in profile."

"Those statues may not be accurate."

"They are pretty good. Most people would settle for them."

"But why would she say it?"

"To put you out of business. That's the oldest way in the world of putting people out of business. Scott, you asked me to tell you the truth and I can tell you a lot more but this is the absolute truth and all you need. You could have gone to see a doctor."

"I didn't want to. I wanted you to tell me truly."

"Now do you believe me?"

"I don't know," he said.

"Come on over to the Louvre," I said. "It's just down the street and across the river."

We went over to the Louvre and he looked at the statues but still he was doubtful about himself.

"It is not basically a question of the size in repose," I said. "It is the size that it becomes. It is also a question of angle." I explained to him about using a pillow and a few other things that might be useful for him to know.

"There is one girl," he said, "who has been very nice to me. But after what Zelda said—"

"Forget what Zelda said," I told him. "Zelda is crazy. There's nothing wrong with you. Just have confidence and do what the girl wants. Zelda just wants to destroy you."

"You don't know anything about Zelda."

"All right," I said. "Let it go at that. But you came to lunch to ask me a question and I've tried to give you an honest answer."

But he was still doubtful.

"Should we go and see some pictures?" I asked. "Have you ever seen anything in here except the Mona Lisa?"

"I'm not in the mood for looking at pictures," he said. "I promised to meet some people at the Ritz bar."

Many years later at the Ritz bar, long after the end of the World War II, Georges, who is the bar chief now and who was the *chasseur* when Scott lived in Paris, asked me, "Papa, who was this Monsieur Fitzgerald that everyone asks me about?"

"Didn't you know him?"

"No. I remember all of the people of that time. But now they ask me only about him."

"What do you tell them?"

"Anything interesting that they wish to hear. What will please them. But tell me, who was he?"

"He was an American writer of the early Twenties and later who lived some time in Paris and abroad."

"But why would I not remember him? Was he a good writer?"

"He wrote two very good books and one which was not completed which those who know his writing best say would have been very good. He also wrote some good short stories."

"Did he frequent the bar much?"

"I believe so."

"But you did not come to the bar in the early Twenties. I know that you were poor then and lived in a different quarter."

"When I had money I went to the Crillon."

"I know that too. I remember very well when we first met."

"So do I."

"It is strange that I have no memory of him," Georges said.

"All those people are dead."

"Still one does not forget people because they are dead and people keep asking me about him. You must tell me something about him for my memoirs."

"I will."

"I remember you and the Baron von Blixen arriving one night—in what year?" He smiled.

"He is dead too."

"Yes. But one does not forget him. You see what I mean?"

"His first wife wrote very beautifully," I said. "She wrote perhaps the best book about Africa that I ever read. Except Sir Samuel Baker's book on the Nile tributaries of Abyssinia.

Put that in your memoirs. Since you are interested in writers now."

"Good," said Georges. "The Baron was not a man that you forget. And the name of the book?"

"*Out of Africa*," I said. "Blickie was always very proud of his first wife's writing. But we knew each other long before she had written that book."

"But Monsieur Fitzgerald that they keep asking me about?"

"He was in Frank's time."

"Yes. But I was the *chasseur*. You know what a *chasseur* is."

"I am going to write something about him in a book that I will write about the early days in Paris. I promised myself that I would write it."

"Good," said Georges.

"I will put him in exactly as I remember him the first time that I met him."

"Good," said Georges. "Then, if he came here, I will remember him. After all one does not forget people."

"Tourists?"

"Naturally. But you say he came here very much?"

"It meant very much to him."

"You write about him as you remember him and then if he came here I will remember him."

"We will see," I said.

There Is Never Any End to Paris

WHEN there were the three of us instead of just the two, it was the cold and the weather that finally drove us out of Paris in the winter time. Alone there was no problem when you got used to it. I could always go to a café to write and could work all morning over a *café crème* while the waiters cleaned and swept out the café and it gradually grew warmer. My wife could go to work at the piano in a cold place and with enough sweaters keep warm playing and come home to nurse Bumby. It was wrong to take a baby to a café in the winter though; even a baby that never cried and watched everything that happened and was never bored. There were no baby-sitters then and Bumby would stay happy in his tall cage bed with his big, loving cat named F. Puss. There were people who said that it was dangerous to leave a cat with a baby. The most ignorant and prejudiced said that a cat would suck a baby's breath and kill him. Others said that a cat would lie on a baby and the cat's weight would smother him. F. Puss lay beside Bumby in the tall cage bed and watched the door with his big yellow eyes, and would let no one come near him when we were out and Marie, the *femme de ménage*, had to be away. There was no need for baby-sitters. F. Puss was the baby-sitter.

But when you are poor, and we were really poor when I had given up all journalism when we came back from Canada, and could sell no stories at all, it was too rough with a baby in Paris in the winter. At three months Mr. Bumby had crossed the North Atlantic on a twelve-day small Cunarder that sailed from New York via Halifax in January. He never cried on the trip and laughed happily when he would be barricaded in a bunk so he could not fall out when we were in heavy weather. But our Paris was too cold for him.

We went to Schruns in the Vorarlberg in Austria. After going through Switzerland you came to the Austrian frontier at Feldkirch. The train went through Liechtenstein and stopped at Bludenz where there was a small branch line that ran along a pebbly trout river through a valley of farms and forest to Schruns, which was a sunny market town with saw-mills, stores, inns and a good, year-around hotel called the Taube where we lived.

The rooms at the Taube were large and comfortable with big stoves, big windows and big beds with good blankets and feather coverlets. The meals were simple and excellent and the dining room and the wood-planked public bar were well heated and friendly. The valley was wide and open so there was good sun. The pension was about two dollars a day for the three of us, and as the Austrian schilling went down with in-flation, our room and food were less all the time. There was no desperate inflation and poverty as there had been in Germany. The schilling went up and down, but its longer course was down.

There were no ski lifts from Schruns and no funiculars, but there were logging trails and cattle trails that led up different mountain valleys to the high mountain country. You climbed on foot carrying your skis and higher up, where the snow was too deep, you climbed on seal skins that you attached to the bottoms of the skis. At the tops of mountain valleys there were the big Alpine Club huts for summer climbers where you could sleep and leave payment for any wood you used. In some you had to pack up your own wood, or if you were going on a long tour in the high mountains and the glaciers, you hired someone to pack wood and supplies up with you, and established a base. The most famous of these high base huts were the Lindauer-Hütte, the Madlener-Haus and the Wiesbadener-Hütte.

In back of the Taube there was a sort of practice slope where you ran through orchards and fields and there was another good slope behind Tschagguns across the valley where there was a beautiful inn with an excellent collection of chamois horns on the walls of the drinking room. It was from behind the lumber village of Tschagguns, which was on the far edge of the valley, that the good skiing went all the way up until you could eventually cross the mountains and get over the Silvretta into the Klosters area.

Schruns was a healthy place for Bumby who had a dark-haired beautiful girl to take him out in the sun in his sleigh and look after him, and Hadley and I had all the new country to learn and the new villages, and the people of the town were very friendly. Herr Walther Lent who was a pioneer high-mountain skier and at one time had been a partner with Hannes Schneider, the great Arlberg skier, making ski waxes for climbing and all snow conditions, was starting a school for Alpine skiing and we both enrolled. Walther Lent's system was to get his pupils off the practice slopes as soon as possible and into the high mountains on trips. Skiing was not the way it is now, the spiral fracture had not become common then, and no one could afford a broken leg. There were no ski patrols. Anything you ran down from, you had to climb up. That gave you legs that were fit to run down with.

Walther Lent believed the fun of skiing was to get up into the highest mountain country where there was no one else and where the snow was untracked and then travel from one high Alpine Club hut to another over the top passes and glaciers of the Alps. You must not have a binding that could break your leg if you fell. The ski should come off before it broke your leg. What he really loved was unroped glacier skiing, but for that we had to wait until spring when the crevasses were sufficiently covered.

Hadley and I had loved skiing since we had first tried it together in Switzerland and later at Cortina d'Ampezzo in the Dolomites when Bumby was going to be born and the doctor in Milan had given her permission to continue to ski if I would promise that she would not fall down. This took a very careful selection of terrain and of runs and absolutely controlled running, but she had beautiful, wonderfully strong legs and fine control of her skis, and she did not fall. We all knew the different snow conditions and everyone knew how to run in deep powder snow.

We loved the Vorarlberg and we loved Schruns. We would go there about Thanksgiving time and stay until nearly Easter. There was always skiing even though Schruns was not high enough for a ski resort except in a winter of heavy snow. But climbing was fun and no one minded it in those days. You set a certain pace well under the speed at which you could climb, and it was easy and your heart felt good and you were proud of the weight of your rucksack. Part of the climb up to the Madlener-Haus was steep and very tough. But the second time you made that climb it was easier, and finally you made it easily with double the weight you had carried at first.

We were always hungry and every meal time was a great event. We drank light or dark beer and new wines and wines that were a year old sometimes. The white wines were the best. For other drinks there was kirsch made in the valley and Enzian *Schnapps* distilled from mountain gentian. Sometimes for dinner there would be jugged hare with a rich red wine sauce, and sometimes venison with chestnut sauce. We would drink red wine with these even though it was more expensive than white wine, and the very best cost twenty cents a liter. Ordinary red wine was much cheaper and we packed it up in kegs to the Madlener-Haus.

We had a store of books that Sylvia Beach had let us take for the winter and we could bowl with the people of the town in the alley that gave onto the summer garden of the hotel. Once or twice a week there was a poker game in the dining room of the hotel with all the windows shuttered and the door locked. Gambling was forbidden in Austria then and I played with Herr Nels, the hotel keeper, Herr Lent of the Alpine ski school, a banker of the town, the public prosecutor and the captain of Gendarmerie. It was a stiff game and they were all good poker players except that Herr Lent played too wildly because the ski school was not making any money. The captain of Gendarmerie would raise his finger to his ear when he would hear the pair of gendarmes stop outside the door when they made their rounds, and we would be silent until they had gone on.

In the cold of the morning as soon as it was light the maid would come into the room and shut the windows and make a fire in the big porcelain stove. Then the room was warm, there was breakfast of fresh bread or toast with delicious fruit preserves and big bowls of coffee, fresh eggs and good ham if you wanted it. There was a dog named Schnauz that slept on the foot of the bed who loved to go on ski trips and to ride on my back or over my shoulder when I ran down hill. He was Mr. Bumby's friend too and would go for walks with him and his nurse beside the small sleigh.

Schruns was a good place to work. I know because I did the most difficult job of rewriting I have ever done there in the winter of 1925 and 1926, when I had to take the first draft of *The Sun Also Rises* which I had written in one sprint of six weeks, and make it into a novel. I cannot remember what stories I wrote there. There were several though that turned out well.

I remember the snow on the road to the village squeaking at night when we walked home in the cold with our skis and ski poles on our shoulders, watching the lights and then finally seeing the buildings, and how everyone on the road said, "Grüss Gott." There were always country men in the *Weinstube* with nailed boots and mountain clothes and the air was smoky and the wooden floors were scarred by the nails. Many of the young men had served in Austrian Alpine regiments and one named Hans, who worked in the sawmill, was a famous hunter and we were good friends because we had been in the same part of the mountains in Italy. We drank together and we all sang mountain songs.

I remember the trails up through the orchards and the fields of the hillside farms above the village and the warm farm houses with their great stoves and the huge wood piles in the snow. The women worked in the kitchens carding and spinning wool into grey and black yarn. The spinning wheels worked by a foot treadle and the yarn was not dyed. The black yarn was from the wool of black sheep. The wool was natural and the fat had not been removed, and the caps and sweaters and long scarves that Hadley knitted from it never became wet in the snow.

One Christmas there was a play by Hans Sachs that the school master directed. It was a good play and I wrote a review of it for the provincial paper that the hotel keeper translated. Another year a former German naval officer with a shaven head and scars came to give a lecture on the Battle of Jutland. The lantern slides showed the movements of the two battle fleets and the naval officer used a billiard cue for a pointer when he pointed out the cowardice of Jellicoe and sometimes he became so angry that his voice broke. The school master was afraid that he would stab the billiard cue through the screen. Afterwards the former naval officer could not quiet himself down and everyone was ill at ease in the *Weinstube*. Only the public prosecutor and the banker drank with him, and they were at a separate table. Herr Lent, who was a Rhinelander, would not attend the lecture. There was a couple from Vienna who had come for the skiing but who did not want to go to. the high mountains and so were leaving for Zurs where, I heard, they were killed in an avalanche. The man said the lecturer was the type of swine who had ruined Germany and in twenty years they would do it again. The woman with him told him to shut up in French and said this is a small place and you never know.

That was the year that so many people were killed in avalanches. The first big loss was over the mountains from our valley in Lech in the Arlberg. A party of Germans wanted to come and ski with Herr Lent on their Christmas vacations. Snow was late that year and the hills and mountain slopes were still warm from the sun when a great snowfall came. The snow was deep and powdery and it was not bound to the earth at all. Conditions for skiing could not be more dangerous and Herr Lent had wired the Berliners not to come. But it was their vacation time and they were ignorant and had no fear of avalanches. They arrived at Lech and Herr Lent refused to take them out. One man called him a coward and they said they would ski by themselves. Finally he took them to the safest slope he could find. He crossed it himself and then they followed and the whole hillside came down in a rush, rising over them as a tidal wave rises. Thirteen were dug out and nine of them were dead. The Alpine ski school had not prospered before this, and afterwards we were almost the only members. We became great students of avalanches, the different types of avalanches, how to avoid them and how to behave if you were caught in one. Most of the writing that I did that year was in avalanche time.

The worst thing I remember of that avalanche winter was one man who was dug out. He had squatted down and made a box with his arms in front of his head, as we had been taught to do, so that there would be air to breathe as the snow rose up over you. It was a huge avalanche and it took a long time to dig everyone out, and this man was the last to be found. He had not been dead long and his neck was worn through so that the tendons and the bone were visible. He had been turning his head from side to side against the pressure of the snow. In this avalanche there must have been some old, packed snow mixed in with the new light snow that had slipped. We could not decide whether he had done it on purpose or if he had been out of his head. He was refused burial in consecrated ground by the local priest anyway, since there was no proof he was a Catholic.

When we lived in Schruns we used to make a long trip up the valley to the inn where we slept before setting out on the climb to the Madlener-Haus. It was a very beautiful old inn and the wood of the walls of the room where we ate and drank were silky with the years of polishing. So were the table and chairs. We slept close together in the big bed under the feather quilt with the window open and the stars close and very bright. In the morning after breakfast we all loaded to go up the road and started the climb in the dark with the stars close and very bright, carrying our skis on our shoulders. The porters' skis were short and they carried heavy loads. We competed among ourselves as to who could climb with the heaviest loads, but no one could compete with the porters, squat sullen peasants who spoke only Montafon dialect, climbed steadily like pack horses and at the top, where the Alpine Club hut was built on a shelf beside the snow-covered glacier, shed their loads against the stone wall of the hut, asked for more money than the agreed price, and, when they had obtained a compromise, shot down and away on their short skis like gnomes.

One of our friends was a German girl who skied with us. She was a great mountain skier, small and beautifully built, who could carry as heavy a rucksack as I could and carry it longer.

"Those porters always look at us as though they looked forward to bringing us down as bodies," she said. "They set the price for the climb and I've never known them not to ask for more."

In the winter in Schruns I wore a beard against the sun that burned my face so badly on the high snow, and did not bother having a haircut. Late one evening running on skis down the logging trails Herr Lent told me that peasants I passed on those roads above Schruns called me "the Black Christ." He said some, when they came to the *Weinstube,* called me "the Black Kirsch-drinking Christ." But to the peasants at the far upper end of the Montafon where we hired porters to go up to the Madlener-Haus, we were all foreign devils who went into the high mountains when people should stay out of them. That we started before daylight in order not to pass avalanche places when the sun could make them dangerous was not to our credit. It only proved we were tricky as all foreign devils are.

I remember the smell of the pines and the sleeping on the mattresses of beech leaves in the woodcutters' huts and the skiing through the forest following the tracks of hares and of foxes. In the high mountains above the tree line I remember following the track of a fox until I came in sight of him and watching him stand with his right forefoot raised and then go carefully to stop and then pounce, and the whiteness and the clutter of a ptarmigan bursting out of the snow and flying away and over the ridge.

I remember all the kinds of snow that the wind could make and their different treacheries when you were on skis. Then there were the blizzards when you were in the high Alpine hut and the strange world that they would make where we had to make our route as carefully as though we had never seen the country. We had not, either, as it all was new. Finally towards spring there was the great glacier run, smooth and straight, forever straight if our legs could hold it, our ankles locked, we running so low, leaning into the speed, dropping forever and forever in the silent hiss of the crisp powder. It was better than any flying or anything else, and we built the ability to do it and to have it with the long climbs carrying the heavy rucksacks. We could not buy the trip up nor take a ticket to the top. It was the end we worked for all winter, and all the winter built to make it possible.

During our last year in the mountains new people came deep into our lives and nothing was ever the same again. The winter of the avalanches was like a happy and innocent winter in childhood compared to the next winter, a nightmare winter disguised as the greatest fun of all, and the murderous summer that was to follow. It was that year that the rich showed up.

The rich have a sort of pilot fish who goes ahead of them, sometimes a little deaf, sometimes a little blind, but always smelling affable and hesitant ahead of them. The pilot fish talks like this: "Well I dont know. No of course not really. But I like them. I like them both. Yes, by God, Hem; I do like them. I see what you mean but I do like them truly and there's something damned fine about her." (He gives her name and pronounces it lovingly.) "No, Hem, dont be silly and dont be difficult. I like them truly. Both of them I swear it. You'll like him (using his baby-talk nickname) when you know him. I like them both, truly."

Then you have the rich and nothing is ever as it was again. The pilot fish leaves of course. He is always going somewhere, or coming from somewhere, and he is never around for very long. He enters and leaves politics or the theater in the same way he enters and leaves countries and people's lives in his early days. He is never caught and he is not caught by the rich. Nothing ever catches him and it is only those who trust him who are caught and killed. He has the irreplaceable early training of the bastard and a latent and long denied love of money. He ends up rich himself, having moved one dollar's width to the right with every dollar that he made.

These rich loved and trusted him because he was shy, comic, elusive, already in production, and because he was an unerring pilot fish.

When you have two people who love each other, are happy and gay and really good work is being done by one or both of them, people are drawn to them as surely as migrating birds are drawn at night to a powerful beacon. If the two people were as solidly constructed as the beacon there would be little damage except to the birds. Those who attract people by their happiness and their performance are usually inexperienced. They do not know how not to be overrun and how to go away. They do not always learn about the good, the attractive, the charming, the soon-beloved, the generous, the understanding rich who have no bad qualities and who give each day the quality of a festival and who, when they have passed and taken the nourishment they needed, leave everything deader than the roots of any grass Attila's horses' hooves have ever scoured.

The rich came led by the pilot fish. A year before they would never have come. There was no certainty then. The work was as good and the happiness was greater but no novel had been written, so they could not be sure. They never wasted their time nor their charm on something that was not sure. Why should they? Picasso was sure and of course had been before they had ever heard of painting. They were very sure of another painter. Many others. But this year they were sure and they had the word from the pilot fish who turned up too so we would not feel that they were outlanders and that I would not be difficult. The pilot fish was our friend of course.

In those days I trusted the pilot fish as I would trust the Corrected Hydrographic Office Sailing Directions for the Mediterranean, say, or the tables in *Brown's Nautical Almanac.* Under the charm of these rich I was as trusting and as stupid as a bird dog who wants to go out with any man with a gun, or a trained pig in a circus who has finally found someone who loves and appreciates him for himself alone. That every day should be a fiesta seemed to me a marvelous discovery. I even read aloud the part of the novel that I had rewritten, which is about as low as a writer can get and much more dangerous for him as a writer than glacier skiing unroped before the full winter snowfall has set over the crevices.

When they said, "It's great, Ernest. Truly it's great. You cannot know the thing it has," I wagged my tail in pleasure and plunged into the fiesta concept of life to see if I could not bring some fine attractive stick back, instead of thinking, "If these bastards like it what is wrong with it?" That was what I would think if I had been functioning as a professional although, if I had been functioning as a professional, I would never have read it to them.

Before these rich had come we had already been infiltrated by another rich using the oldest trick there is. It is that an unmarried young woman becomes the temporary best friend of another young woman who is married, goes to live with the husband and wife and then unknowingly, innocently and unrelentingly sets out to marry the husband. When the husband is a writer and doing difficult work so that he is occupied much of the time and is not a good companion or partner to his wife for a big part of the day, the arrangement has advantages until you know how it works out. The husband has two attractive girls around when he has finished work. One is new and strange and if he has bad luck he gets to love them both.

Then, instead of the two of them and their child, there are three of them. First it is stimulating and fun and it goes on that way for a while. All things truly wicked start from an innocence. So you live day by day and enjoy what you have and do not worry. You lie and hate it and it destroys you and every day is more dangerous, but you live day to day as in a war.

It was necessary that I leave Schruns and go to New York to rearrange publishers. I did my business in New York and when I got back to Paris I should have caught the first train from the Gare de l'Est that would take me down to Austria. But the girl I was in love with was in Paris then, and I did not take the first train, or the second or the third.

When I saw my wife again standing by the tracks as the train came in by the piled logs at the station, I wished I had died before I ever loved anyone but her. She was smiling, the sun on her lovely face tanned by the snow and sun, beautifully built, her hair red gold in the sun, grown out all winter awkwardly and beautifully, and Mr. Bumby standing with her, blond and chunky and with winter cheeks looking like a good Vorarlberg boy.

"Oh Tatie," she said, when I was holding her in my arms, "you're back and you made such a fine successful trip. I love you and we've missed you so."

I loved her and I loved no one else and we had a lovely magic time while we were alone. I worked well and we made great trips, and I thought we were invulnerable again, and it wasn't until we were out of the mountains in late spring, and back in Paris that the other thing started again.

That was the end of the first part of Paris. Paris was never to be the same again although it was always Paris and you changed as it changed. We never went back to the Vorarlberg and neither did the rich.

There is never any ending to Paris and the memory of each person who has lived in it differs from that of any other. We always returned to it no matter who we were or how it was changed or with what difficulties, or ease, it could be reached. Paris was always worth it and you received return for whatever you brought to it. But this is how Paris was in the early days when we were very poor and very happy.